MARCH,
WOMEN, MARCH

MARCH, WOMEN, MARCH

LUCINDA DICKENS HAWKSLEY

ANDRE
DEUTSCH

THIS IS AN ANDRÉ DEUTSCH BOOK

This edition published in 2013 by André Deutsch Limited
A division of the Carlton Publishing Group
20 Mortimer Street
London
W1T 3JW

10 9 8 7 6 5 4 3 2 1

A CIP catalogue for this book is available from the British
Library

ISBN: 978 0 233 00373 3

Printed and bound by CPI Group (UK) Ltd, Croydon, CR0 4YY

Contents

Acknowledgments

I would like to thank for following people for their help with this book, both in the writing of it and the sales and publicity people who will start their work on it now it's published. First and foremost I want to say thank you to my editors Gemma Maclagan Ram and Vanessa Daubney, also to my agent Broo Doherty and to Dr Helen Pankhurst for agreeing to write the foreword. In addition, I would like to thank (in alphabetical order): Suji Barnett, Sally Beattie, Becky Cross, Clare Double, Nicole Ettinger, Ilya Fisher, Jim Greenhough, Dominique Kenway, Claire Martin, Natasha McEnroe at the Florence Nightingale Museum, Frank McNamara, Lynsey Metcalfe, Piers Murray-Hill, Tamsin Pickeral (for horse-racing information), Vanessa Potts, Catherine Rubinstein, Amara Thornton, Susan Wheatley, Kate Wheeler and Barbara-Ann Zimmerman. With thanks also to the staff at the BBC Archive, British Library, British Museum, British Newspaper Archives, Greater London Authority archive, London Library, Museum of London, National Archives at Kew, National Gallery, National Horse Racing Museum, People's History Museum, Warwick University archives and The Women's Library.

Foreword by
Dr Helen Pankhurst

What is the story behind the changing landscape of British society and the place that women play within in? How did it change from one in which women were not even second-class citizens, with no legal identity of their own, no economic, political and sexual and reproductive rights, to the situation in which, by the end of the 1920s, many rights, including the pivotal one of equal voting rights, had been won?

The answer is rooted in the determination of some centrally important protagonists and the battles that they waged, refusing to accept women's traditional lot, often because of their own particular circumstances, but also because they saw that a better alternative was needed, not only for themselves but for others. It is a story of how individuals became leaders, how they made their mark on history, because of their beliefs, and their passion, which in turn fired the imagination of others. The call for change, "for liberty and justice" was magnified and a momentum generated. Detractors dug their heels in and tried to hold on to the status quo, but too many people took up the baton and together, over time, they shook the system fundamentally, pushing through one change after another.

Too often nowadays the complexity and multi-dimensional aspect of the mid-Victorian and Edwardian women's movement in the UK is boxed into a few iconic images and words. High up on the list are the Suffragettes, "Purple, white and green", the Pankhursts, militancy and the "Cat and Mouse Act". These words and images have been absorbed into the British psyche and collective memory – they define, but in doing so, they also shrink the women's rights movement.

There were so many other women who pioneered a whole raft of social, political and economic changes and who are now largely forgotten. We need to remember them. They included Caroline Norton, whose case contributed to the rights of women to divorce their husbands and earn their own money; Barbara Leigh Smith and Bessie Rayner Parkes, who worked to change the way women and girls were treated through education, health and legal reforms; Elizabeth Garrett, who tackled the obstacles stopping her from working as a doctor and opened the door for other women to do so, and Elizabeth Siddal and Jane Morris who spearheaded a move away from the constricting attire of the cage crinoline, the bustle and the corset through dress reform as part of the Rational Dress movement. Also pivotal – and in their case still largely remembered – were Florence Nightingale and Marie Stopes. There were also hundreds of organizations and unions supporting individual pioneers and contributing to the overall tide of change.

The women's movement in the United Kingdom also needs to be understood in terms of the influences on and by other countries, particularly the United States, but also Europe and New Zealand and Australia, two former colonies where women got the vote in 1892 and 1902 respectively, well before women in the British "motherland". As well as the international dimension, the women's movement also existed within a context of other social, political and economic campaigns. In terms of its message and methods, it had links with the anti-slavery campaign, and was sometimes part of, and sometimes against, those calling for wider male suffrage and equality. The women's movement did not arise in a vacuum but was, and continues to be, part of a more complex story of change.

Looking at the Suffragettes, they themselves were sometimes united and sometimes divided by class, age, geography, family, race, political affiliation and attitudes to male involvement in the movement, to militancy and to styles of leadership. Yet the power of the movement lay in the numbers it could muster, in the style and pageantry it used to make its case, in the courage and endurance of its members, and in the stunts that ordinary women initiated, such as the first stone-throwing by two schoolteachers, Mary Leigh and Edith New and the first hunger strike by an artist, Marion Wallace Dunlop, actions that were then taken on by the wider movement.

Lucinda Hawksley's *March, Women, March* provides a very readable and much needed overview of the story of women's emancipation starting in the Victorian era and ending in the late 1920s. It does so to a large extent through the words and writings of the pioneers and others of their time and with a commentary that makes the connections and provides background information. It brings to life individual struggles and how these contributed to the movement – how the determination of a few and the persistent support of the many, despite huge setbacks, slowly but surely, led to a transformed British landscape in which "liberty and justice" became more than just a dream.

Dr Helen Pankhurst
Granddaughter of Sylvia, Great-granddaughter of Emmeline Pankhurst

Chapter One

To many people in Britain, the phrase "the women's movement" is synonymous with the campaign undertaken by the suffragettes. Yet the struggle for gender equality began long before the Pankhurst family rose to the fore, and many decades before the *Daily Mail* coined the word "suffragette" as an insult.

In 1791, the radical thinker and activist Thomas Paine wrote a book that would change the course of masculine history. In *The Rights of Man*, the author argued that all men should be entitled to vote because they were all equal in the eyes of God. A year later, the author and feminist Mary Wollstonecraft published a response that would do the same for women's history as Paine's book had done for men's. At the beginning of *A Vindication of the Rights of Women*, Wollstonecraft addresses her female readers with the words:

"My own sex, I hope, will excuse me, if I treat them like rational creatures, instead of flattering their fascinating graces, and viewing them as if they were in a state of perpetual childhood, unable to stand alone."

A Vindication of the Rights of Women may not have brought about an immediate political result, and its author may not have received universal adulation during her lifetime, but by the time women in Britain were finally permitted the basic human right of voting, Wollstonecraft's book was accepted as a turning point in gender equality.

Issues of women's rights were inextricably bound up with other aspects of human rights as a whole, and many of the earliest campaigners for women's rights were also involved in the anti-slavery campaign. The idea of equality for all and "universal suffrage" (the right to vote for all adult citizens) was a concept that seemed obvious to the few and yet utterly abhorrent to those in power. The men who were entitled to vote – and in the late 18th century remarkably few were given that entitlement, the franchise in Britain, as in many other nations, being based on a certain level of property ownership – were understandably resistant to change. They knew that if men of all classes were given the vote, the accepted "old order" would change forever. Those men who were entitled to vote were socially acquainted with those in power, and they did not consider that those of the lower classes would have any idea of how to run a country – or, at least, how to run a country in a manner that those currently in power would have found acceptable.

To most of these men, the idea that a woman might have a desire to talk about and to influence politics was laughable. Women of all social classes were viewed as third-class citizens, less important than men or even their own male children. As far as those in power were concerned – whether that power was in the House of Lords or in the humble home – women were not to be consulted when it came to politics and law-making. Women were, as many women of Mary Wollstonecraft's era were keen to point out, little better than slaves. Mary Wollstonecraft described marriage for women as nothing more than being "legally prostituted".

A popular masculine response to such agitation was expressed by the politician James Mill, who declared in the 1820s that women did not need the vote because their husbands and/or fathers would make political decisions on their behalf and would thereby ensure women were protected. Wollstonecraft had complained of women being kept in "perpetual childhood" and that was precisely what Mill was advocating. In his essay entitled "Government", he grouped together women and children, arguing that neither were in need of individual representation:

> *"One thing is pretty clear, that all those individuals whose interests are indisputably included in those of other individuals, may be struck off [the list of those who should be granted the vote] without inconvenience. In this light may be viewed all children, up to a certain age, whose interests are involved in those of their parents. In this light, also, women may be regarded, the interest of almost all of whom is involved either in that of their fathers or in that of their husbands."*

Some years later, James Mill's son John Stuart Mill would become an active supporter of women's suffrage.[1] That particular paragraph of his father's work made him cringe; he described it as "the worst he ever wrote".

James Mill's derisibly naïve assumption that all women in Britain lived happy lives, never mistreated by their male relatives, was lampooned in his own lifetime. In 1825, partly in response to Mill's essay, William Thompson and Anna Wheeler collaborated on the publication *An Appeal of One Half of the Human Race*. The pamphlet continued Mary Wollstonecraft's theme: that women in England and elsewhere were oppressed by archaic marriage laws and that true happiness could only

---

1. John Stuart Mill fell in love with an influential early feminist, Harriet Taylor, a member of the Radical Unitarians. When the couple met, Taylor was already married with children. To enable her relationship with Mill to thrive without humiliating her husband, Harriet set up a second home, where she could spend time with Mill. Her husband, John Taylor, tolerated the relationship. In 1851, two years after her husband's death, Harriet married John Stuart Mill.

be found when men and women were able to live in a "partnership between equals". The pamphlet began with the exhortation:

> "Women of England! Women, in whatever country ye breathe – wherever ye breathe, degraded, awake! Awake to the contemplation of the happiness that awaits you when all your faculties of mind and body shall be fully cultivated and developed; when every path in which ye can exercise those improved faculties shall be laid open and rendered delightful to you, even as to them who now ignorantly enslave and degrade you.... But you are not so degraded. The unvaried despotism of so many thousand years has not so entirely degraded you, has not been able to extinguish within you the feelings of nature, the love of happiness and of equal justice."

Within a few years of the publication of Thompson and Wheeler's pamphlet, it seemed as though gender equality in Britain might actually be in the offing. Throughout Europe, great changes had been taking place, and stories of rebellion and revolution had become a regular topic of conversation in the newspapers. Ever since the bloodthirsty French Revolution of 1789–99, monarchies and governments had lived in fear of the power of the masses, and in Britain in the 1820s and 1830s, the question of entitlement to vote was a cause that refused to go away and was becoming increasingly embittered. Prior to 1832, only 3 per cent of the male population of Britain was permitted to vote. It was becoming apparent that a vast proportion of the other 97 per cent was growing increasingly angry; it was also becoming apparent that those with power were likely to find themselves in serious danger from those without. The government had begun to realize that it would need, at least, to start talking about a more egalitarian system of voting.

The year 1832 saw the "great" Reform Bill – a bill that promised much more than it ended up providing and which, thanks to the efforts of the

MP Henry Hunt, brought the issue of female emancipation a minuscule step closer. Although Hunt's efforts would come to nothing, he introduced, as part of the Reform Bill preparation, a petition to grant the vote to some women. The women he had proposed should be enfranchised were a few unmarried female property owners (the petition did not propose to franchise all unmarried women with property, only those at the very top of the social and financial scales). For months, those few women affected by the petition waited with bated breath, truly thinking that they might, at last, gain the right to influence the laws under which they lived. In the end, although the bill enfranchised many more men than the original 3 per cent, not a single woman was awarded the entitlement to vote. Hunt's petition had, however, brought the idea of female suffrage right into the heart of the House of Commons. From that moment onward, the issue refused to go away.

On 14 December 1837, the MP John Temple Leader spoke at a debate in the House of Commons. His speech included the words: "As it stands at present, the law is entirely in favour of the husband and oppressive to the wife. A man ... may be drunken, immoral, vicious and utterly brutalized.... The wife, in such a case, has no redress." He added, "There are hundreds of women now suffering in silence, pining for the children whom a stern law has torn from them ... eagerly hoping that the representatives of the people will save them from the terrible alternative which forces them to choose between being the abject slaves of a brutal husband or being deprived of the very sight of their own children." One such woman was preparing to begin a very long fight, which would culminate in sweeping changes to the British legal system.

Chapter Two

"Women often strive to live by intellect ... if they are but allowed to live in it."

Florence Nightingale, "Cassandra", 1852

When, towards the end of the 19th century, the women of the Garrett and Fawcett families took up the issue of female suffrage, the movement would begin to be associated with upper-class, often aristocratic women, yet in the early 19th century this was not the case. The earliest exponents of gender equality came not from the drawing rooms of Mayfair but from the factory floors of those towns most affected by the Industrial Revolution. When the Chartist Movement drew up its People's Charter in 1838, a clause on women's suffrage was included; unfortunately it was taken out in revised versions of the charter, but its presence in the first draft showed how much earlier the need for sexual equality was being discussed in the working classes than in the majority of upper-class homes.

In 1843, the government published the *Report of the Poor Law Commissioners on the Employment of Women and Children in Agriculture*, which looked at the problems encountered by working men whose wives also worked. As historian Ray Strachey would later note in her book on the fight for women's suffrage *The Cause* (1928), the report proved that women working in the fields enjoyed better health than women working in the home, but it also seemed to suggest that such women were responsible for their poor benighted husbands taking to drink and becoming bad husbands. There was no suggestion that when both a husband and wife worked outside the home, duties inside the home should be shared equally. It was expected that the woman would do everything at home, as well as earning a weekly wage, and that her husband would feel aggrieved at being neglected in favour of his own children:

> *"The general conclusion as to the physical condition of women engaged in agriculture is that it is generally better than that of the same class not employed ... her health is better ... [but] the husband is a sufferer from his wife's absence from home. There is not the same order in the cottage, nor the same attention paid to his comforts as when his wife remains in the home all day. On returning from her labour she has to look after the children and her husband may have to wait for his supper. He may come home tired and wet; he finds his wife has arrived just before him, and she must give her attention to the children; there is no fire, no supper, no comfort, and he goes to the beer shop."*

The report's overriding message was that women should be sacrificed for the sake of men and for the family as a whole. The findings that women's health was being improved by working outside the home were considered of secondary importance to the fact that their menfolk were suffering through a lack of "wifely" domestic care.

In the world of work, women who laboured alongside their male counterparts were aware of the great inequalities between the two genders' treatments and wage packets – but they were also fully aware of how vital they were to local industry. Through earning their own money, these women had a much greater sense of freedom than women who lived in wealthy homes. Despite having the appearance of being much wealthier than their working-class counterparts, such women were unable to do or buy anything without relying on their husbands for every coin they spent.

As the century drew on, the fight for gender equality also began to be discussed widely by women of the middle and upper classes. Part of the reason for this was the infamous plight of one intelligent and vocal woman from their ranks. She spoke out – and continued to speak until she was listened to – because her life was blighted by the viciousness of her husband's cruelty and the misogynist laws which allowed him legal rights to continue to abuse her.

The woman whose experiences would lead to direct changes in laws affecting women and children was born Caroline Elizabeth Sarah Sheridan on 22 March 1808, a granddaughter of the dramatist Richard Brinsley Sheridan. During the Sheridan children's childhoods, the fact that their grandfather was still so famous and his memory so revered seemed to bode well for their futures. Added to which, their mother had been a "famous beauty", and Caroline and her sisters inherited their mother's celebrated looks. The family was, however, always on the brink of financial disaster (just as the playwright himself had often been), and the situation worsened following the death of the father, Tom Sheridan, of tuberculosis, when Caroline was a child. From an early age, Caroline realized that she would need to help the family finances and she began to practise her inherited literary skills. A worry that preoccupied all the female children in the family was the knowledge that, somehow, they needed to marry well despite having no dowries.

When Caroline was 16, she was taken to the home of Lord and Lady Grantley, where she was noticed by George Norton, the younger brother of Lord Grantley. Although Caroline had little interest in him, Norton pursued her. Caroline's mother (who had already forbidden one "unsuitable" romance with a young army officer) encouraged him to do so. Unfortunately for Caroline, there seemed to be no other willing suitor to marry a young woman without a dowry – no matter how pretty or intelligent she was. Caroline was also pressingly aware of her need to relieve her family from having to support her financially. George Norton pursued the uninterested young woman for two years and, aware that his older brother was still childless which meant George might well inherit not only the estate but the title as well, Mrs Norton pushed relentlessly for the marriage. Eventually, Caroline found herself agreeing to marry a man she barely knew. Not only were her ideals and expectations entirely different from those of her future husband but, perhaps equally seriously, they did not agree on politics. The Sheridan family had long been supporters of the Whig party – and Caroline was a politically aware and politically interested young woman of more than average intelligence. In contrast, the Nortons were staunch far-right Tories, with a long-established hatred of Whig policies and politicians.

The wedding of Caroline Elizabeth Sarah Sheridan and George Chapple Norton took place on 30 July 1827 in the fashionable church of St George's in Hanover Square, London. In contrast to accepted tradition, the bride was on time, while the groom was late. The wedding ceremony marked the beginning of decades of misery and abuse for the beautiful, intelligent young woman whose early career had begun with such promise. By the time of the wedding, Caroline had begun to make her name as a writer, earning a meagre living from her works, but this ability to earn her own money was to prove useless as soon as she placed her signature on the wedding register.

From the very start of her marriage, the extended Norton family was unimpressed by Caroline. George's siblings and siblings-in-law found her self-confidence and independence galling. These were traits that George sought to beat out of his young wife (a bride so young she had needed to be married with her mother's special consent) from the earliest days of their marriage. Caroline had grown up in a house where discussion and intellectual conversation was commonplace but, from the first days of their marriage, whenever she attempted to reason with, or to reprimand, her husband, he would repay her with physical violence. He became particularly vicious when drunk, which was a common occurrence. Shortly after the wedding, Caroline learned to be afraid of her husband. Later she would write an account of their marriage in which she related:

"We had been married about two months, when ... we were discussing some opinion Mr Norton had expressed; I said, that 'I thought I had never heard so silly or ridiculous a conclusion.' This remark was punished by a sudden and violent kick; the blow reached my side; it caused great pain for several days, and being afraid to remain with him, I sat up the whole night in another apartment."

Another account of his violence related an incident when her husband was criticizing a friend of the family: "I defended the lady spoken of when he suddenly sprang from the bed, seized me by the nape of the neck, and dashed me down on the floor." When her sister and brother-in-law rushed to her aid, having heard the violent noises coming from Caroline's room, George Norton tried to refuse them entry to the bedroom. Eventually her sister's husband "burst the door open and carried me downstairs" to safety, but despite this one act of bravado her relatives knew they were powerless to stop such abuse from happening again.

In 1839, the writer and women's campaigner Sarah Stickney Ellis published a book entitled *The Women of England: Their Social Duties and Domestic Habits* in which she wrote about the inequalities within marriage and the need for women to subjugate their true personalities in order not to anger their husbands. A quotation from her book seems to illustrate the problems Caroline Norton experienced: "In the case of a highly gifted woman, even where there is an equal or superior degree of talent possessed by her husband, nothing can be more injudicious, or more fatal to her happiness, than an exhibition of the least disposition to presume upon such gifts."

Seeking escape from her unhappiness, during the first year of her marriage, Caroline Norton turned to writing poetry. Her first collection was published – anonymously at first – as *The Sorrows of Rosalie*. A couple of years later, she published a second volume of poems, *The Undying One and Other Poems*. Both were well received, as was her first play, *The Gypsy Father*, and by the early 1830s the name Caroline Norton was being talked about in every literary salon in town. According to the law, however, a married woman was not entitled to her own earnings, so all the money Caroline made from her writing went directly to her husband. She knew that no matter how much money she made, she would never be entitled to spend a penny more than her husband allowed. By agreeing to marry, she had become enslaved to her husband and his family.

Within a few years of their marriage, Caroline had become the mother of three sons, whom she adored. Fletcher was born in 1829, Thomas (always known by his second name of Brinsley) in 1831 and William in 1833. Baby William was named after a friend of the Nortons, Lord Melbourne.[1] The Nortons had first met Melbourne, who was then Home Secretary, in 1831. He would be voted in as Prime Minister in 1834. One of Lord Melbourne's heroes was Richard Brinsley Sheridan, and he had been friends with Caroline's father some years earlier, so he was thrilled to meet the playwright's granddaughter. Despite detesting Lord Melbourne's politics, George Norton was in need of advancement in his own career and determined to take advantage of the situation. He pushed his wife to improve their acquaintance with Melbourne and insisted she become more friendly with him. To Caroline, this order from her husband was no hardship: she had liked and trusted Melbourne from the start, she knew he had been a friend of her father (whom she barely remembered) and she was keen to renew a family friendship.

Through his wife's friendship with Lord Melbourne, George Norton was secured an extremely well-paid position as a magistrate in East London. Despite earning several thousand pounds a year and receiving all his wife's earnings, George Norton found it impossible to live within his means and Caroline was thrust back into the financial fears of her childhood. Her response was to keep writing, as a result of which her fame continued to increase. She was also moving in interesting

---

1. Lord Melbourne's wife, Lady Caroline Lamb, had scandalized society and cuckolded her husband by her affair with Lord Byron.

literary circles, including befriending the writer Mary Shelley, author of *Frankenstein* (widow of the Romantic poet Percy Bysshe Shelley and daughter of the deceased Mary Wollstonecraft). Caroline's success and literary lifestyle incensed her husband, who, although happy to live off his wife's earnings, was resentful of her ability to earn money and her desire to have a life outside of their home.

The Nortons' marriage became increasingly unhappy and abusive, with George as resentful of Caroline's love for their children as he was of her obvious dislike and distrust of him. In 1835, Caroline finally left her husband, terrified of his abusive behaviour – but as she was pregnant and desperately missing her sons, she returned to the family home. This decision to return would later be used against her in court. Shortly after her return home, Caroline miscarried her fourth baby, almost certainly because of her husband's violent treatment of her. By this time George was bored with his wife and his marriage. He was also aware that Caroline was becoming increasingly infatuated with Lord Melbourne – a friendship she clung to with growing desperation as her husband became increasingly abusive. Norton now had everything he needed to rid himself of Caroline, to wound her more viciously than he had ever wounded her before, and to bring down a man whose politics he had always despised (despite his protestations of friendship when he had needed Melbourne's help).

In 1836, George Norton ordered his servants to take his three sons from their London home and not to reveal their whereabouts to the boys' mother. A distraught Caroline searched in desperation for her sons; when she finally discovered their whereabouts, she was refused access to them. The law was entirely on her husband's side: children were legally the "property" of the father. Because Norton then accused his wife of infidelity, she was disallowed, by law, any contact with her children. There was no physical proof of Norton's allegations, but in 1836, a man's word against a woman was as good as evidence and any woman of "blemished character" was considered unfit to be around children. As a result, Caroline was denied any maternal rights. George Norton's sadism was allowed to continue unbounded – as the law stood, it was his legal right to treat his wife with utter lack of concern

– nor was she allowed any access to the money she had earned. In effect she could be rendered penniless and childless, and there was no law in Britain that could help her.

The person with whom Caroline was accused of having an affair was the Prime Minister. In the legal parlance of the day, Lord Melbourne was accused of having had "criminal conversation with Mrs Norton". It was not Caroline who was being sued: Norton was suing Lord Melbourne for sullying his "property" – a wife being merely a possession of her husband's. The case was brought to court in June 1836 and, although Norton would eventually lose the case and Melbourne would be exonerated, Caroline Norton was to suffer for the rest of her life.

As a result of the court case and the ensuing scandal, Caroline lost her children, one of her closest friends (Melbourne was too embarrassed to continue to associate with her after the accusations, despite her desperate pleas and constant letters) and her all-important reputation. She was also in desperate financial straits: no matter how hard she worked or how successful her writing became, she remained reliant on her brutal, vengeful, estranged husband for every penny, and he taunted her for decades by spending as much as possible of her earnings and keeping her in financial difficulties whenever he could. By law, Norton needed only to ensure that Caroline did not become a burden on the country's finances. As long as he acceded to that stipulation, the law would not intervene. To add to what was already an overwhelming misery, Caroline was devastated by the news that one of her young sons had been killed shortly after the separation, following a fall from a horse. She wrote the following account of how she found out: "Mr Norton allowed the child to lie ill for a week before he sent to inform me. Lady Kelly (who was an utter stranger to me) met me at the railway station. I said, 'I am here – is my boy better?' 'No,' she said, 'he is not better – he is dead.' And I found, instead of a child, a corpse already coffined."

Caroline Norton felt that she had lost everything, yet instead of giving up, she determined to fight. The tragedy of her life would have a directly positive impact for generations of women to come.

In 1837, one year after the Norton v. Melbourne scandal, the people of Britain welcomed a new monarch. When 18-year-old Princess Victoria was declared Queen on the death of her uncle King William IV, it was hoped that a kinder, more compassionate era would begin. For several generations, British subjects had been unimpressed by their monarchy. The Hanoverian kings George I and George II had shown little interest in their people and, although King George III and especially his kindly wife Queen Charlotte seemed promising monarchs, when he was declared insane and their profligate son became Prince Regent, whispers of revolution and republicanism began to infiltrate through every layer of society. The Prince Regent enjoyed a brief reign as King George IV before being succeeded by his brother King William IV – a man who tried to present a respectable front, but who, everyone knew, had fathered 10 illegitimate children with the actress Mrs Jordan (although he and his wife, Queen Adelaide, were unable to produce one healthy heir). By the time Queen Victoria came to the throne, the people of Britain were in need of a monarch to admire.

The government, led by Lord Melbourne (who was one of Queen Victoria's most trusted early advisors), was all too aware that the people of Britain might well follow the example of those in France and America, rejecting the monarchy altogether. The young Queen knew, from the beginning of her reign, that she needed to become a very different type of sovereign from her uncles and grandfather. From the beginning, Queen Victoria sought to appease her people and, for the first couple of decades, she was extremely successful. Yet she was not as popular a monarch as children are widely taught that she was in school today: a total of seven assassination attempts would be made upon her life and, following the death of her husband, when she plunged herself into four decades of mourning, she would become increasingly unpopular. During this period, the reputation of the royal family would be buoyed up not by the Queen but by her children, who stepped in to fulfil the public roles she refused. In the early years of her reign, however, Queen Victoria was joyfully received by her public as a young woman who, it was hoped, might bring about important and wide-reaching changes. The women of Britain were particularly thrilled to have a female monarch after so many years of distant Germanic kings. It was believed by many – erroneously, as history would relate – that under the reign of a queen, women would finally achieve suffrage.

Caroline Norton was one of those who felt that the accession of a female monarch would lead to a more compassionate Britain. She also felt that the Queen, who married in 1840 and rapidly entered motherhood (much too rapidly as far as Victoria herself was concerned), would be sympathetic towards her own plight. Caroline threw herself into study of the law and began to write impassioned letters to her monarch, highlighting not only her own situation but that of so many women in Victoria's England.

In the year before Queen Victoria's marriage, Caroline had been influential in helping to bring about a change in the law. The passing of The Custody of Infants Act 1839 allowed a woman to petition through the courts for custody of her children under the age of seven and for access to her children who were over the age of seven. The original bill, drafted in 1838 with the help of Thomas Talfourd MP, was firmly rejected by the House of Lords (having been accepted by the House of Commons). The bill was rewritten with the amendment that a mother's right to be given custody of her children (under the age of seven) would be decided on an individual basis – each woman's case would have to obtain the specific agreement of the Lord Chancellor and he would only give it if the woman "was of good character".

Although in the most censorious areas of London society Caroline was considered *persona non grata*, there were also many people who felt she had been cruelly used and had sympathy with her. As the years following the notorious court case passed and Caroline's literary fame continued to grow, the number of her supporters increased. As early as 1838, a Welsh journalist reviewing her poetry referred to her as "the talented and ill-used Caroline Norton". In 1840, almost all the newspapers were keen to publish a letter she had written after her husband had attempted once more to blacken her name with yet another court case; it was a letter which spoke eloquently of her misery at losing her children, of her husband's "bitter" treatment of her and her "perpetual torment", and in which she appealed "for protection against annoyances which I may be ridiculed for calling 'persecutions', but which are nevertheless intolerable and disgraceful". The newspapers were firmly on the side of Caroline Norton, but the law was inexorably on the side of her husband.

Literary appreciation of Caroline Norton was extensive. In 1848, the novelist Anne Brontë (who, for some reason, is today the least celebrated of the remarkable literary Brontë sisters) published her second novel, *The Tenant of Wildfell Hall*. It is an astonishing story, well ahead of its time in many ways. Its heroine is the mysterious Mrs Graham, or Helen, whose sudden appearance in a small community causes excited discussion. Her attempts to stay out of society and her perceived "mollycoddling" of her young son cause great excitement – and rumours soon abound that she is not a widow and that her son is in fact the illegitimate child of her landlord. The narrator, Gilbert Markham, a young man who falls in love with her, gradually comes to know the truth about her life. It transpires that Helen is living at Wildfell Hall under a pseudonym, having fled her abusive alcoholic husband in order to be able to keep custody of her son – and that her landlord, Frederick Lawrence, is actually Helen's brother (they have to keep their relationship a secret so her estranged husband is not alerted to her whereabouts). Anne Brontë was almost certainly inspired by Caroline Norton's life when writing her novel. She uses it to deprecate the different treatment meted out by parents to male and female children, as well as by society to men and women. She writes about the folly of educating boys to one standard and girls to another – suggesting that men and women will never be able to live in marital harmony while such disparity exists. Anne Brontë's opinions would be echoed a decade later in the writings of the American author Amelia Bloomer, who wrote: "Nothing has tended more to the physical and moral degradation of the race than the erroneous and silly idea that woman is too weak, too delicate a creature to have imposed upon her the more active duties of life, – that it is not respectable or praiseworthy for her to earn a support or competence for herself."

> *"Keep both heart and hand in your own possession, till you see good reason to part with them; and if such an occasion should never present itself, comfort your mind with this reflection, that though in single life your joys may not be very many, your sorrows, at least, will not be more than you can bear. Marriage may change your circumstances for the better, but, in my private opinion, it is far more likely to produce a contrary result."*
>
> **The Tenant of Wildfell Hall**

In 1850, following the death of William Wordsworth and a discussion of who should be named the new Poet Laureate, a journalist from *The Daily News* argued that, "under the rule of an enlightened Queen, it were fit that the laureateship should devolve on a lady, and Elizabeth Barrett Browning, or Caroline Norton, is named as fully deserving that honour." In the event, Alfred Tennyson was chosen, but the fact that Caroline Norton's name was even being talked about in association with such an honour demonstrated how much literary and social power she had attained, through her refusal to accept her husband's and the legal system's brutal subjugation and keep quiet about her plight. The majority of women in her situation, as demonstrated by Anne Brontë's heroine, would have been forced to move out of their own society and into a secretive life elsewhere after the kind of scandal Caroline Norton had excited, but she was determined not to lie low and hide away. Caroline was furious, and righteously so, and she wanted to make a difference to both her own and all women's history. Alice Acland, an early biographer of Caroline Norton, wrote in 1948: "She was out of tune with the spirit of her age and she suffered accordingly."

Chapter Three

"There was a great deal of romantic feeling about you ... [in] the Crimea. And now you work on in silence, and nobody knows how many lives are saved by your nurses in hospitals ... how many natives of India ... have been preserved from famine ... by the energy of a sick lady who can scarcely rise from her bed."

Letter to Florence Nightingale from Benjamin Jowett,
Master of Balliol College, Oxford, 1879

When the poet Coventry Patmore married Emily, he believed that he had found the ideal Victorian wife. As such, he wrote a poem in her honour calling upon all women to strive towards Emily's level of perfection and immortalized her as the "Angel in the House" (1854). According to Patmore, the perfect wife had to put her husband's happiness first in everything and continue to worship him long after his death, sacrificing her own happiness in order to preserve his memory. The Angel in the House must be passive, self-sacrificing, meek, submissive, charming, pious, full of selfless devotion, sympathetic, devoid of any power of her own – and chastely pure, of course. In 1931, Virginia Woolf would comment that "killing the Angel in the House was part of the occupation of a woman writer". Although Patmore was concise about everything that the ideal wife should do and provide for her husband, he was less clear about what a man's role should be in order to make his wife equally happy, seeming to feel that this lack of awareness was a forgivable masculine caprice. His poem contains the lines:

> "Man must be pleased; but him to please
> Is woman's pleasure, down the gulf
> Of his condoled necessities
> She casts her best, she flings herself...
> She leans and weeps against his breast,
> And seems to think the sin was hers;
> And whilst his love has any life,
> Or any eyes to see her charms,
> At any time, she's still his wife,
> Dearly devoted to his arms;
> She loves with love that cannot tire;
> And when, ah woe, she loves alone,
> Through passionate duty love springs higher,
> As grass grows taller round a stone."

While Emily Patmore was preparing to take on the role of a domestic angel, and Caroline Norton was suffering without her children and composing letters to the Queen, a young woman had been growing up on a wealthy family estate in Hampshire. She was feeling increasingly desperate about the enforced uselessness of her life – a life she felt was meant to be useful and extraordinary. In the early 1850s, Florence Nightingale completed an extended essay entitled "Cassandra" (which Virginia Woolf would later describe as being akin to the author having "shrieked aloud in agony"). The essay deals with the plight of women and reveals Nightingale's fury with what she perceived as the stifling, imprisoning Victorian family – a world away from Coventry Patmore's image of the domestic "angel".

Nightingale's essay is intelligent and angry. The author asks:

> *"Why ... have women passion, intellect, moral activity*
> *– these three – and a place in society where no one of*
> *the three can be exercised?... in the conventional society,*
> *which men have made for women, and women have*
> *accepted ... [women]* <u>*must*</u> *act the farce of hypocrisy, the*
> *lie that they are without passion – and therefore what else*
> *can they say to their daughters, without giving the lie to*
> *themselves?"*

Some years earlier, Florence Nightingale had told her family that she had received a vocation, a religious calling telling her she should become a nurse. Her wealthy parents were appalled that not only was she intending to have a career, but that she wanted to work in a degrading profession which would require her to have in-depth knowledge of the male, as well as female, anatomy. Hospitals were also dirty and dangerous places to be in at the time. Despite fierce opposition, Nightingale had remained resolute and, against her family's wishes, trained as a nurse. By the time of writing "Cassandra", she was 32 years old and, having rejected offers of marriage, was considered too old to be marriageable. She was working in London as a superintendent at The Establishment for Gentlewomen During Illness in Upper Harley Street, yet in her personal life she continued to be stifled by her family's wishes, their overbearing disapproval and their social conditioning. As she wrote in "Cassandra":

> *"Women are never supposed to have any occupation*
> *of sufficient importance not to be interrupted, except*
> *'suckling their fools'; and women themselves have*
> *accepted this, have written books to support it, and have*
> *trained themselves as to consider whatever they do as*

31

not of such value to the world or to other, but that they can throw it up at the first 'claim of social life'. They have accustomed themselves to consider intellectual occupation as a merely selfish amusement, which it is their 'duty' to give up for every trifler more selfish than themselves."

With the outbreak of the Crimean War in 1854, Nightingale found the summit of her vocation. She was asked by Sidney Herbert, a personal friend and the Secretary at War, to take an expedition of female nurses (all volunteers) to work in an army-run military hospital at Scutari, on the shore of the Bosphorus. Although many historians now criticize Nightingale's medical record (her early nursing methods, especially those employed in Scutari, are often ridiculed by modern medical experts), there is no questioning her impact on the perception of women as being both capable and intelligent, and how much she and her opinions helped with the inexorable move forward towards gender equality.[1]

While Florence Nightingale was being lauded by journalists as "the Lady with the Lamp", Caroline Norton was completing her most important and influential work. In 1855, she sent to Queen Victoria

---

1. Until her death at the age of 90 on 13 August 1910, Florence Nightingale continued to work tirelessly on matters concerning public health and sanitation, both in Britain and overseas, and on changing the way that military hospitals were run. She raised funds for nurses to be trained and for women to have rewarding careers, setting up the first proper school for nurses, the Nightingale Training School at St Thomas' Hospital in London. Most of these operations she directed from her bedroom, having suffered from ill-health and taken to her bed while still a relatively young woman. After returning from the Crimea to the stultifying atmosphere of Victorian England, she was never again quite able to summon the energy that had typified her life in Scutari. A museum dedicated to her life and work has been established at St Thomas' Hospital.

a 30,000-word pamphlet that detailed, in full, the inequality between men and women in Victorian England. In *A Letter to the Queen on Lord Cranworth's Marriage and Divorce Bill* Caroline Norton wrote that she wanted "to point out the grotesque anomaly which ordains that married women shall be 'non-existent' in a country governed by a female Sovereign". It included the following hard-hitting points, impossible, as it turned out, for the Queen to continue to ignore:

- *"A married woman in England has no legal existence: her being is absorbed in that of her husband. Years of separation or desertion cannot alter this position. Unless divorced by special enactment in the House of Lords, the legal fiction holds her to be 'one' with her husband, even though she may never see or hear of him. She has no possessions, unless by special settlement; her property is his property."*

- *"An English wife cannot make a will. She may have children or kindred whom she may earnestly desire to benefit; – she may be separated from her husband, who may be living with a mistress; no matter: the law gives what she has to him, and no will she could make would be valid."*

- *"An English wife cannot legally claim her own earnings. Whether wages for manual labour, or payment for intellectual exertion, whether she weed potatoes, or keep a school, her salary is the husband's; and he could compel a second payment, and treat the first as void, if paid to the wife without his sanction."*

- *"An English wife may not leave her husband's house. Not only can he sue her for 'restitution of conjugal rights', but he has a right to enter the house of any friend or relation with whom she may take refuge, and who may 'harbour her', – as it is termed, – and carry her away by force, with or without the aid of the police."*

- *"If the wife sue for separation for cruelty, it must be 'cruelty that endangers life or limb', and if she has once forgiven, or, in legal phrase, 'condoned' his offences, she cannot plead them; though her past forgiveness only proves that she endured as long as endurance was possible."[2]*

- *"If her husband take proceedings for a divorce, she is not, in the first instance, allowed to defend herself. She has no means of proving the falsehood of his allegations. She is not represented by attorney, nor permitted to be considered a party to the suit between him and her supposed lover, for 'damages'."*

- *"If an English wife be guilty of infidelity, her husband can divorce her so as to marry again; but she cannot divorce the husband a vinculo [absolutely, fully], however profligate he may be."*

- *"She cannot prosecute for a libel. Her husband must prosecute; and in cases of enmity and separation, of course she is without a remedy."*

- *"She cannot sign a lease, or transact responsible business."*

Caroline Norton also pointed out that these laws were different from those that governed the lives of women in Scotland. She reiterated several times that the law favoured only the rich and enfranchised – "it is not law for the poor", she wrote more than once in the letter. Her own plight was also outlined:

> "Now again, I say, is or is not this a ridiculous law (if laws be made to conduct to justice)? I cannot divorce my husband, either for adultery, desertion, or cruelty; I _must_ remain married to _his name_; _he_ has ... a right to everything I have in the world – and I have no more claim upon _him_, than any one of your Majesty's ladies in waiting, who are utter strangers to him! I never see him:– I hear of him only by attacks on my reputation:– and I do not receive a farthing of support from him."

After almost two decades of pleading by such a persistent and eloquent subject, the Queen was finally moved to act. Caroline's words were too well-informed, too truthful and too impassioned to be ignored. It had taken 18 years since the Queen had come to power, but Caroline Norton had finally forced her monarch to accept the truth and to take a stand on the appalling plight of every other woman in the country.

On 28 August 1857, An Act to Amend the Law relating to Divorce and Matrimonial Causes in _England_ was passed by Parliament. It was declared that the act (usually known as the Divorce and Matrimonial Causes Act) would become law on 1 January 1858. Before the 1857 act,

---

2. This was precisely the argument used against Caroline Norton: despite the fact that her husband beat her viciously, because she had returned to the family home after initially leaving him (she returned when she was pregnant for the fourth time and desperately missing her sons), she was deemed to have agreed to, even colluded in, his treatment of her.

a man could only obtain a divorce by suing another man (or more than one) for "criminal conversation", as George Norton had attempted to do to Lord Melbourne. Such a case assumed that the wife as property had been "damaged" by adultery (or rape) and had therefore lost the property's worth. The case was more about suing for financial costs than about the dissolution of a marriage. The 1857 act allowed a man to petition for divorce on the grounds of adultery, for similar reasons: if he could prove his wife had taken a lover, she was effectively threatening his property and estate, the reasoning being that any children of the marriage might not be his and therefore he might have no legitimate heirs to inherit the family fortune or he might unwittingly leave his property to the son of another man.

Under the new act, women were also given the right to petition for divorce – but there was still a sad lack of equality. Not only did a woman have to prove her husband's adultery, as a man did if he was the one seeking the divorce, but there were a number of other conditions attached. As well as being adulterous, a man must also have committed bigamy or incest, have treated his wife with cruelty (and the terms of what constituted cruelty had to be "life-threatening" and were minutely defined) or have deserted her. In legal parlance, the law stated that, for a woman to obtain a divorce from an adulterous husband, he must, in addition to the adultery, have been guilty of: "incestuous Adultery, or of Bigamy with Adultery, or of Rape, or of Sodomy or Bestiality, or of Adultery coupled with such Cruelty as without Adultery would have entitled her to a Divorce *a Mensa et Thoro* [a legal separation short of full divorce], or of Adultery coupled with Desertion without reasonable Excuse, for Two Years or upwards". If a woman was proved to have committed adultery, she lost all legal rights to her children; if a man was proven to have committed adultery, he was still allowed to see his children.

The act did, however, introduce an important clause for women's independence. It allowed a wife who had been deserted by her husband to earn her own money, and that money (up to a certain amount) would now be protected from any claims the deserting husband might make.

The Divorce and Matrimonial Causes Act of 1857 was not without its inequalities and problems. The only grounds for divorce remained proven adultery; a couple who were unhappily married were not permitted to apply for a divorce simply on the grounds of incompatibility. Despite this, it was recognized by the public that many marriages were dissolved for precisely that reason. In 1859, *The Times* reported wryly: "The crowded state of the Divorce Court shows what an enormous amount there was of matrimonial misery." Nor did a divorce under the 1857 act permit remarriage. A divorced man or woman was still only allowed to remarry if their ex-spouse was dead and they could be considered widowed.

Furthermore, the act did not benefit all women – the cost of a divorce case meant that it was of little help to any but the wealthiest – but it was a vital stepping stone on the path to female emancipation. In 1867, Lydia Becker, a woman who would grow to great prominence in the cause of female suffrage, commented on the state of marriage in Britain and what seemed to be a utopian wish for equality: "I think that the notion that the husband ought to have the headship or authority over his wife, is the root of all social evils... Husband and wife should be co-equal. In a happy marriage there is no question of 'obedience.'"

Another Matrimonial Causes Act would be passed in 1878, which would allow women married to violent husbands to obtain what was, in effect, a judicial separation, and which – vitally – gave them custody of their children. It was not a full divorce and, even if they obtained a divorce, remarriage was still not an option. Most importantly, however, the 1878 act "protection order" was inexpensive, unlike a divorce case, which meant it enabled women of all classes to achieve protection from violent husbands and custody of their children. Women would not receive equal rights in the divorce court until 1923.

Chapter Four

"A woman's body belongs to her husband; she is in his custody, and he can enforce his right by a writ of habeas corpus."

Barbara Leigh Smith, from *A Brief Summary in Plain Language of the Most Important Laws Concerning Women*, 1854

In the 1840s, two women had begun what would prove to be not only an enduring friendship but an important link in the chain that forged the women's movement. When Barbara Leigh Smith[1] and Elizabeth ("Bessie") Rayner Parkes became friends, they realized that they shared a desire to improve the lot of women less fortunate than themselves. Both women came from radical-thinking homes; they grew up in progressive Unitarian families where the opinions of both men and women were valued. The Unitarian faith was a pivotal part of the fight for female equality. Other prominent Unitarians, who would be described today as early feminists, included the writers and reformers Elizabeth Gaskell,

---

1. Barbara was first cousin to Florence Nightingale – although, as Barbara and her siblings were illegitimate, they were not welcomed into the Nightingale family.

Frances Power Cobbe and Harriet Martineau. Through her travels and her writing, Harriet Martineau also helped to forge valuable links between the women's movements in Britain and America.[2] Martineau had been attempting to bring about change in women's lives since the 1830s. While Caroline Norton was agitating for reform in the law courts, Martineau had been writing about the position of women and querying, as Mary Wollstonecraft had done, whether marriage was advisable for everyone, a hugely controversial stance to take. Despite the forcefulness of her early writing, Martineau's contribution to the women's movement was less obvious during the middle period of the 19th century as she was hampered by ill health. Her writings, however, remain influential and fascinating, as she agitated not only for change where women were concerned but also for the abolition of slavery and for a fair education system open to both genders and all economic classes. She moved in very political circles and was a supporter of the Whig party; as such, her writings often dealt with what were considered the "masculine" subjects of economics and the need for political changes.

Both Barbara Leigh Smith and Bessie Rayner Parkes also sought to bring about changes to the way they saw girls and women being treated, becoming campaigners for education reform, health reform, legal reform and the anti-slavery movement. They were committed to the cause of female suffrage long before the subject began making regular appearances in the newspapers – although Barbara was much more vocal on the subject than her friend. Bessie was cautious about allying herself openly with a cause that was so politically inflammatory. Both women wrote articles and essays for local magazines and radical newspapers, and encouraged other women to do the same. Bessie's writing included a pamphlet entitled *Remarks on the Instruction of Girls*; Barbara's included *A Brief Summary of the Most Important Laws Concerning Women* and *Reasons for the Enfranchisement of Women*.

---

2. It was following his first trip to America in 1842 that the novelist Charles Dickens changed his faith to become a Unitarian, having been influenced by speeches he had listened to and what he saw as the Unitarians' genuine desire to bring about social change.

Bessie was also a poet and Barbara a promising artist.[3] Historian and leading suffragist Ray Strachey would later write, "There seems to have been something particularly vigorous about Barbara Leigh Smith, who was taken by George Eliot as the model for Romola. Tall, handsome, generous and quite unselfconscious, she swept along.... Life was a stirring affair for Barbara. Everything was before her."

Barbara and Bessie were remarkable for being 19th-century women who lived their lives without pandering to the accepted constraints. They went away to Germany together – travelling unchaperoned, something that was considered scandalous – and chose to dress for comfort (relinquishing corsets and other restrictive clothing) long before the Rational Dress Movement became fashionable or accepted. In 1858, the two women founded the *English Woman's Journal*, a monthly magazine. Articles published in the journal placed it at the forefront of the campaigns that called for women's suffrage and for married women to be allowed to own – and retain – property. Together with an influential group of friends, they attempted to introduce to Parliament a Married Women's Property Act in 1857, although it was unsuccessful. Barbara married in the same year as this failed act; her husband was a French physician named Eugène Bodichon.[4] The couple journeyed to America on their honeymoon, where Barbara contacted leading women's rights campaigners and attended discussions. When she returned to England, she was buoyed up by the vitality of the women's suffrage campaigns in Philadelphia and Boston, and determined to set up similar associations in London. A few years later, she helped found the Kensington Ladies' Discussion Society. At one of their meetings, Barbara gave a talk on female suffrage which led to the founding of the Women's Suffrage Committee – a precursor to all the influential suffrage groups that would follow in the next half-century.

---

3. Barbara would also go on to co-found Girton College, Cambridge.

4. Ten years after Barbara's wedding, Bessie also married a Frenchman, Louis Belloc. Their son was the poet Hilaire Belloc and their daughter Marie Belloc Lowndes was a successful novelist.

Despite the Bodichons' marriage being one of equality, Barbara experienced at first hand all the legal restrictions she had been campaigning against. When the *English Woman's Journal* was created a limited-liability company, Barbara, the major shareholder, was forced to buy her shares in the name of her unmarried sister Anne, because married women were forbidden to own shares. In addition to founding the magazine, Barbara and Bessie also founded the Langham Place Women's Group, whose members were as philanthropic and proactive as themselves, and counted among their number the novelist George Sand, the poet Adelaide Procter and the activist Emily Davies.

The group met at the journal's offices, 19 Langham Place, in central London. The offices were funded by the philanthropist Theodosia, Lady Monson, and included a large meeting room for the committee, a reading room and a coffee shop. The hope was that women of all social classes would be inspired to use the offices as a meeting place and safe haven. It was a place in which to organize philanthropic work as well as being welcoming to those in need of help. Out of the group grew the Society for the Promotion of the Employment of Women, the Female Middle-Class Emigration Society and the Ladies' Sanitary Association (at that date one out of every three children born in London died in infancy, the majority due to poor sanitation), and several of the members also set up evening classes to pass on their knowledge and to educate other women. The last issue of the *English Woman's Journal* was published in 1864, but the group continued to work together. In 1866, Barbara Leigh Smith Bodichon and Emily Davies were among those who initiated the very first official campaign calling on Parliament to address the issue of women's suffrage. Among the men who supported their cause was John Stuart Mill (the son of the anti-suffrage politician James Mill).

One of the issues that concerned women was the tendency to deride all women who fought against the status quo as "mad" or "hysterical". Influential and misogynous groups within the medical profession devoted their time and training to declaring that any woman who did not conform was insane – and there were always doctors to be found who were willing to collude with angry husbands wanting to rid themselves of "troublesome" wives by committing them to an asylum. A woman could be declared insane for showing too much emotion, for being overtly sexual or flirtatious, or simply because her husband (or another male relative in legal control of her) claimed that she was mad. Legislation did attempt to prevent men from simply getting rid of an unwanted wife by shutting her away in an asylum – when divorce became possible, "insanity" was not permissible as a reason for a husband to divorce his wife – but for many women, the fear of "Bedlam" (the name of the most notorious asylum) was an ever-present spectre.

The issue was addressed by Wilkie Collins in his 1860 novel *The Woman in White*, with a plot that hinged upon the perceived insanity and incarceration of a young woman. The eponymous woman dressed all in white appears at the very start of the novel; we later discover her name is Anne Catherick and that she has escaped from an asylum. She bears an astonishing resemblance to a young woman named Laura Fairlie, an heiress whose husband, Sir Percival Glyde, marries her only for her money. Following the timely (and expected) death of Anne Catherick, Glyde buries Anne as Laura and has the real Laura locked up in the asylum, claiming she is Anne and is under the delusion that she is Lady Glyde. The convoluted plan was enacted so that Sir Percival would inherit Laura's fortune. The book, billed as a sensational thriller, was published in instalments in the weekly magazine *All The Year Round* (under the editorship of Charles Dickens). It became an immediate literary phenomenon, with men and women equally under the spell of Collins' prose. It also had its detractors, among them the politician and writer Edward Bulwer Lytton, who derided Collins' novel as "great trash". There was a personal reason why Bulwer Lytton found the novel so disquieting: two years previously, he had had his own wife, Rosina, admitted to an asylum. The couple had already been separated for over 20 years and their relationship had deteriorated to such an extent that they detested each other with a bitterness that spilled over into public life. After Rosina publicly denounced her estranged husband as a liar, he had her declared insane. It took just three weeks in the asylum for Rosina to be declared sane and be released.[5] The scandal was still keenly in the public consciousness when Wilkie Collins published the first instalment of *The Woman in White*.

> *"This is the story of what a Woman's patience can endure,*
> *and what a Man's resolution can achieve."*
> **Woman in White**

The subject of female insanity was something that would resurface repeatedly throughout the women's movement campaign, with regular accusations of "madness" hurled at suffragists (as campaigners for women's suffrage were termed) and, later, suffragettes (their more activist sisters). It was a subject that fascinated the Victorian mind, and local newspapers published statistics of how many people in the region had been declared insane. In 1874, the *Huddersfield Chronicle* reported that there had been a "remarkable increase of female insanity during the last ten years" (something the reporter attributes mostly to a change in the laws concerning the selling of alcohol). Twelve years later, in 1886, the *London Standard* published a summary of the lunacy figures for the county of Kent, where there was a reported "large increase in female insanity. At the present time there are in the two asylums [Burming and Chartham] as many as 1,225 females to 882 males."

Even well into the 20th century, a woman could be committed to a lunatic asylum simply for having had sex outside of marriage – in many cases the sex was non-consenting, yet these victims of rape were not seen as victims. When a man raped a woman it was almost always considered the woman's fault; she should have *done* something

---

5. Rosina was a successful writer, who used her wit and intelligence to wage a furious campaign against her husband and to reveal scandal about his private life.

to prevent it, or not have been found in such a place where rape was possible, or should not have behaved "inappropriately". The family of a woman who had been raped was considered shamed by the action, and instead of being outraged on her behalf, frequently fathers or brothers blamed the woman for bringing shame on their family name. Many women who were raped were considered sexually precocious, and the rape itself, and the resulting trauma, was often used as an excuse to have a woman declared insane and locked up.

In the middle of the 19th century, however, a number of women were campaigning to have sexual assault recognized as a crime against women. This movement gathered momentum throughout the second half of the 1860s, when many in the Langham Place Women's Group joined a small but powerful group of people protesting about a new series of government Acts. In 1864, the first Contagious Diseases Act had been passed. The second act was passed in 1866 and a third in 1869. In recent years, the government and health professionals had been airing their concerns about the prevalence of sexually transmitted infections (STIs), something that was causing a particular problem amongst military personnel. In their wisdom, the law-makers decided that it was the "diseased" women who should be targeted, not the men. In true Victorian double-standard style, they deemed it revolting that a woman should be sexually active but normal and natural for a heterosexual man to be so, and the language used around these acts was highly emotive. The Acts laid down laws by which a "common prostitute" (a term that was used in the act but never defined legally) could be arrested, forcibly examined for sexual diseases and imprisoned for up to nine months.

The Contagious Diseases Acts gave policemen *carte blanche* to arrest any woman whom they suspected. The acts were most concerned with stamping out STIs in naval and garrison towns, and 18 such towns were specified in the acts. This meant that any woman who lived within 10 miles (16 kilometres) of any of the named towns was in danger of being arrested. Many innocent women who happened to be walking alone or behaving in a manner the police deemed "unseemly" were detained and sexually abused under the Acts. Examinations were supposed to be carried out only at a medical facility, but many women claimed they had been "inspected" for sexual diseases by policemen; the act gave men the legal right to touch women in a sexual manner without requiring their consent.

Although the acts were initially brought in to "protect" military men (who were not permitted to marry), they began to have wider implications, playing on the emotive subject of prostitutes being a danger to family life and to blameless women. The problem with STIs was not confined solely to unmarried military men, and the increasing number of married women infected by errant husbands was becoming a medical problem. The message that such Acts of Parliament conveyed was that it was not men who slept with prostitutes who were a danger to family life; rather the danger came from the infected women, working as prostitutes, who passed on their sexual diseases to men, who then gave those diseases to their unwitting and "innocent" wives. The onus was never on men to stay faithful to their spouses, but on prostitutes not to become infected in the first place (no one ever seems to have queried who might have passed on the infection to a prostitute in the first instance).

It was expected that the very nature of these acts would discourage women in polite society from discussing such a subject, yet the mood in Britain was changing and women of all classes were shocked into action by the injustice and sexual violence of the acts. Florence Nightingale was one of the first prominent campaigners against the Contagious Diseases Act and she was joined by the vociferous campaigners Josephine Butler (née Grey) and Elizabeth Wolstenholme (who would become prominent in the campaign for women's suffrage).

The most famous critic of the acts was Josephine Butler, who risked both her own and her husband's reputations by taking on the government over such a taboo subject as venereal disease. George Butler was an academic who later became a church minister and who shared his wife's desire to make the world a better place. Together they campaigned for the abolition of slavery and worked to improve the lives of "friendless" women. After they left Oxford and moved to Liverpool, the couple set up housing projects for local women in need, often taking desperate women into their own home.[6] Much of Josephine's desire to change the society in which she lived grew out of her own suffering following the death of her youngest child, a daughter who died from a tragic accident at home. Josephine recognized that this experience shaped her campaigning zeal: she wanted to help those who were even more unhappy than herself because, she wrote, "I understand. I, too, have suffered."

By the mid-1860s, Josephine Butler was already a well-respected writer, so she was the ideal influential person to lead the campaign against the Contagious Diseases Acts. Her campaign spanned all classes, reaching inside Buckingham Palace as well as to the persecuted women on the streets of Liverpool. Princess Louise, the sixth child of Queen Victoria and Prince Albert, wrote a letter of support to Josephine Butler, offering to help with her work. Louise, still a young woman and not yet married, was a sculptor who longed to live a non-royal life. She would remain interested in controversial causes throughout her long life,[7] but her family were appalled that she had even thought about allying herself with such a taboo cause. Even her older brother, the scandalous Bertie (future King Edward VII), who was usually her ally, would not back his sister on this subject. Louise was forced by her mother to return the book Josephine Butler had sent to her and to relinquish her earlier-expressed desire to help with the campaign. Undeterred by Queen Victoria's displeasure, Josephine Butler, as leader of the Ladies' National Association for the Repeal of the Contagious Diseases Acts, toured the country making speeches condemning the acts and the

---

6. One of Josephine Butler's causes was the education of women. She was appointed President of the North of England Council for the Higher Education of Women and was influential in persuading Cambridge to set up a college exclusively for female students, Newnham College.

7. Princess Louise lived until 1939 and took on a huge number of charitable roles. She was especially interested in furthering the education of girls and woman, determined that access to education should not be determined by gender or finances. Princess Louise founded the Girls' Public Day School Trust, whose schools continue today.

oppression of women they permitted. That any woman should choose to speak in public about sex horrified Victorian sensibilities – but it was exactly that kind of reaction that Butler knew would help her cause. She and her colleagues were successful: the Contagious Diseases Acts were repealed in 1886.

While the furore was raging about the Contagious Diseases Acts, another young woman was seeking to change the future of the medical profession itself. Elizabeth Garrett, the daughter of a successful pawnbroker, had grown up in East London in a liberal and intelligent home. Her parents paid for a good education and it was realized early that Elizabeth had exceptional academic talent. After meeting Dr Elizabeth Blackwell, the first woman in the United States to graduate as a doctor, Elizabeth Garrett knew what she wanted to do in life and she strove to make it happen. She attempted to be accepted into medical school in England but, despite having attained academic excellence, she was refused on the grounds of her gender and forced to enrol as a nurse instead. While studying as a nurse, she began attending medical students' classes but, following complaints from male students, she was banned from attending any more. She did, however, pass the Society of Apothecaries' exam in 1865, thereby having all the relevant qualifications to become a doctor, yet still being disallowed from studying to become one. Thwarted in London, Elizabeth Garrett moved to Paris where she attained a medical degree. Upon returning to England, she was still refused permission to be registered as a doctor.

Shortly after her return from France, Elizabeth married James Anderson. The following year, she established The New Hospital for Women in central London.[8] Throughout her marriage and the births of her children, she continued to campaign for women's rights and for

---

8. The New Hospital for Women later became the Elizabeth Garrett Anderson Hospital. In 2008 this was closed, and its maternity and neonatal services were moved to the Elizabeth Garrett Anderson Wing of the new University College Hospital.

her right to be recognized by the medical profession. In 1876, thanks to her tireless efforts, the law was finally changed to allow women to train as doctors.

All of these pioneering mid-Victorian women paved the way for the suffragists and suffragettes of the future. By the middle of Queen Victoria's reign, the age of the suffragist had begun, spearheaded by Elizabeth Garrett Anderson's younger sister Millicent. The situation they were dealing with would be chronicled some decades later by women's rights campaigner Helena Swanwick in her autobiography *I Have Been Young*. In it she commented on why she joined the suffrage campaign: "A boy might be a person but not a girl.... All my brothers had rights as persons; not I."

Chapter Five

"The only measure which can satisfy us is one which shall secure to women the same rights to their own property and earnings which are enjoyed by men."

Elizabeth Wolstenholme, from a letter to *The Times*,
September 1870

By the second half of the 1860s, women all over the British Isles had started to form groups with the aim of making their voices heard. These groups included the Manchester Society (founded by Elizabeth Wolstenholme), which would soon galvanize a number of other small local suffrage societies to join together and form the Manchester National Society for Women's Suffrage (the MNSWS[1]), the London Society for Women's Suffrage and the Ladies' London Emancipation Society. The MNSWS set up a new journal, the *Women's Suffrage Journal*, which was edited by Lydia Becker. Many of the suffrage campaigners had played an active part in the anti-slavery movement, so the new groups naturally looked to the same types of ideas as had been used for that campaign.

---

1. This group would undergo several name changes, becoming the North of England Society for Women's Suffrage (NESWS) and then the Manchester Society for Women's Suffrage.

They drew up petitions, held meetings, produced pamphlets and other propaganda, and held fundraising events. Much of the money raised was put to active local use, helping women in financial need and supporting local educational and health services for women and children. In 1867, there was great excitement about a new Reform Bill presented to Parliament, including an amendment proposed by John Stuart Mill in favour of female suffrage. As before, their hopes were dashed as Mill's amendment was thrown out by his peers.

In addition to John Stuart Mill, there were a number of other men who felt very strongly about the need for change and the necessity for equality. In 1870, a radical lawyer named Richard Pankhurst drafted a bill in favour of women's suffrage and presented it to Parliament. It received the same response as Mill's had done. In the same year, however, another bill that Pankhurst drafted was also presented – and this one was passed. His successful bill was the first Married Women's Property Act. Once this crucial act was passed, married women were permitted to keep their earnings and any property inherited or acquired after marriage – although it did not go as far as to permit women to keep any property they owned at the time of their marriage; that still passed immediately to the husband.

Two of the most important clauses in the bill included:

- *"1. The wages and earnings of any married woman acquired or gained by her after the passing of the Act in any employment, occupation, or trade in which she is engaged or which she carries on separately from her husband, and also any money or property so acquired by her through the exercise of any literary, artistic, or scientific skill, and all investments of such wages, earnings, money or property, shall be deemed and taken to be property held and settled to her separate use, independent of any husband to whom she may be married; and her receipts alone shall be a good discharge for such wages, earnings, money, and property."*

- *"10. Property by this Act declared to be the separate property of a married women, shall not be subject to the control or interference of her husband, or to his debts, except such debts as may have been contracted by her or his agent for the support of herself or their children, to which excepted debts it shall be a subject. A married woman may maintain an action in her own name for the recovery of any wages, earnings, money, and property by this Act declared to be her separate property."*

The act was welcomed by the women's suffrage societies, although they were aware (as was Richard Pankhurst) that it did not go far enough. In addition, it still ignored the subject of women getting the vote and, of necessity, it was mostly beneficial to the country's wealthiest women, those who were able to own property. Eager that the politicians should not be allowed to think that the issue was over, Lydia Becker and Elizabeth Wolstenholme wrote a letter to *The Times* in which they announced that the Married Women's Property Committee would continue to campaign for a "truly comprehensive property law". The patriarchal world of the newspapers was incensed by what they perceived as this lack of gratitude on the part of the women. On Saturday, 20 August 1870, the *Morning Chronicle* published a scathing attack on Becker and Wolstenholme, the gist of the article being that most women would be far too stupid to be able to understand or make use of what the act offered them anyway:

"There are, indeed, some Englishwomen, of whom Miss Becker is the representative and leader, who so far from being grateful for this measure, choose to regard it rather as a riveting of the chains which enthral their sex than as an act of emancipation. We would hope, however, that even they will accept it as an instalment

of justice; and we are confident that the great mass of English matrons, when they have studied its provisions, and have considered the extent to which they render them independent of their husbands, will not be so much disposed to ask for increased powers as they will be perplexed to know how they are to use those which the Act confers upon them."

The journalist went on to express concern about the great problems he believed the act would cause in everyday domestic life, direly predicting that helping women even to such a small extent would cause only a lack of harmony and misery in the marital home now that the sacred order had been disturbed:

"In truth, its provisions are so revolutionary of the relations between husband and wife, that we should look with considerable uneasiness upon its probable operation if we did not feel assured that in an overwhelming majority of cases it will have no operation at all. We do not deny that the Act is in many respects necessary. Of the 800,000 married women who are said to be earning wages of their own there is no doubt that a considerable percentage are not blessed with sober and industrious husbands.... For good or evil it is a measure of the highest importance. It may effect a total change in the domestic life of England, and though we believe that in the great majority of cases it will be practically a dead letter, we cannot conceal from ourselves that there are many households in which its tendency will be rather to increase differences than to lessen them."

Another important act was also passed in 1870: the Elementary Education Act, which allowed some female ratepayers (property owners only) to vote for and serve on school boards. It was a very small step forward, but at least a tiny minority of women had moved a modicum closer to voting for their government.

Chapter Six

"The fear I have is, lest we should invite her unwittingly to trespass upon the delicacy, the purity, the refinement, the elevation of her own nature, which are the present sources of its power."

Letter on female suffrage from Prime Minister
William Gladstone to Samuel Smith MP, 1892

By the end of the 1860s, there were three major centres of the women's suffrage movement in Britain: London, Edinburgh and Manchester. Bristol and Birmingham soon joined in and there were meetings being held in other cities, towns and villages all over the country. These women (and their male supporters) kept in touch with each other about activities and activism and – although there would grow to be several major divisions within the suffrage movement – at the beginning there was a shared vision between all the suffrage groups, each determined that women should be taken seriously both in Parliament and in their local communities.

In 1871, however, the first serious split in the suffrage movement took place. This gave the newspapers and those men who were opposed to female suffrage the excuse they needed to laugh at the prospect of women attempting to seek empowerment, when they couldn't even agree amongst themselves. The squabble between different regions and between women with different views on what suffrage would – and should – mean gave their opponents plenty of opportunity to poke fun at the warring women, as was characterized in a verse published in the satirical magazine *Punch* claiming that women who wanted the vote were the ugly ones with nothing else in their lives (those who were lacking in womanly "charms"):

> *"Beauty has claims for which she fights*
> *At ease with winning arms*
> *The women who want woman's rights*
> *Want mostly, women's charms."*

A couple of years after *Punch*'s scathing comments about modern women, the writer Marian Evans published what is widely perceived as her greatest novel, *Middlemarch*, under the pseudonym by which she is better known, George Eliot. The novel was remarkable for being written by a woman and yet not being what Eliot herself would describe as a despised "mind-and-millinery" novel. Eliot was bored with what was deemed suitable writing and subject matter for a woman. She wanted to write a serious book with themes applicable to everyday life, which would be read and appreciated by men and women alike. In order to be taken seriously, Eliot decided that she (as the Brontë sisters had decided some decades earlier) would submit her manuscript under a male pseudonym. It is interesting to ponder whether *Middlemarch* would have been the literary phenomenon it became had it been published under the name Marian Evans.

> *"It is an uneasy lot at best to be what we call highly taught and yet not to enjoy; to be present at this great spectacle of life and never to be liberated from a small, hungry, shivering self – never to be fully possessed by the glory we behold, never to have our consciousness rapturously transformed into the vividness of a thought, the ardour of passion, the energy of an action, but always to be scholarly and uninspired, ambitious and timid, scrupulous and dim-sighted."*
>
> **Middlemarch**

It was not only in a literary sense that Eliot broke the rules: she lived her life in an unconventional manner too. In 1851, when she was in her early thirties, she met the critic and philosopher George Henry Lewes. He was married, but he and his wife Agnes Jervis had what they called an "open marriage", and Agnes was already sexually involved with other men. In 1854, Lewes and Eliot began living together. Divorce was not an option, so Lewes and his wife remained legally married, though living apart, but Lewes and Eliot described their relationship as a "marriage". The situation scandalized Eliot's friends and family, not least because her upbringing had been strictly religious.[1]

---

1. Despite her status during her lifetime as one of Britain's greatest novelists, George Eliot was denied a place in Westminster Abbey's Poets' Corner when she died in 1880, largely because of her relationship with George Henry Lewes and her marriage, after Lewes' death, to a much younger man. This was despite the fact that, 10 years earlier, Charles Dickens had been buried there with great ceremony, even though he was known to have separated very bitterly from his wife and – something less widely acknowledged but well known to his friends – had been having a relationship with the young actress Ellen Ternan for the final 13 years of his life.

Eliot also wrote articles, and in the early 1850s had been editor of the *Westminster Review*. She had a sharp wit and a sharp tongue, and was often accused of being too censorious towards her own sex. What Eliot could not abide was the idea that women were fit only for writing formulaic love stories with gentle womanly themes. In an article for the *Westminster Review* entitled "Silly Novels by Lady Novelists" she describes exactly what she finds most galling about female literature, mostly to do with impossibly perfect heroines. It is a sentiment that is often echoed in the present day in relation to models, as seen in magazines and on screen, airbrushed and digitally "enhanced" and thereby giving an erroneous and unattainable "ideal" of female beauty. Eliot described the archetypal heroine of contemporary novels in the following way: "Her eyes and her wit are both dazzling; her nose and her morals are alike free from any tendency to irregularity; she has a superb contralto and a superb intellect; she is perfectly well-dressed and perfectly religious; she dances like a sylph and reads the Bible in the original tongues."

> *"She is grace itself; she is perfectly lovely and accomplished. That is what a woman ought to be; she ought to produce the effect of exquisite music."*
> **Middlemarch**

The sentiment in this article echoes back to Jane Austen's heroine Elizabeth Bennett (in *Pride and Prejudice*), who gives a spirited rebuttal on hearing the list of what Mr Darcy perceives to be essential accomplishments for the ideal woman:

> *"Then," observed Elizabeth, "you must comprehend a great deal in your idea of an accomplished women."*
>
> *"Yes; I do comprehend a great deal in it."*
>
> *"Oh! certainly," cried his faithful assistant, "no one can be really esteemed accomplished, who does not greatly surpass what is usually met with. A woman must have a thorough knowledge of music, singing, drawing, dancing, and the modern languages, to deserve the word; and besides all this, she must possess a certain something in her air and manner of walking, the tone of her voice, her address and expressions, or the word will be but half deserved."*
>
> *"All this she must possess," added Darcy, "and to all this she must yet add something more substantial, in the improvement of her mind by extensive reading."*
>
> *"I am no longer surprised at your knowing only six accomplished women. I rather wonder now at your knowing any."*
>
> **Pride and Prejudice**

Middlemarch was subtitled "A Study of Provincial Life". Its characters are not overly remarkable, wealthy or aristocratic heroes and heroines, but everyday people living within a small community. Of its large cast, the most intriguing women in the novel – despite sometimes being frustrating to the minds of modern readers – are Dorothea Brooke and Mary Garth, women separated by social class yet who, eventually, share one common goal: to live their lives as intelligent, independent-minded women.

While George Eliot was creating some of the strongest female characters in contemporary fiction, women all over the country were starting to rise up not only against their male, law-making "oppressors" but also against one another. One of the first splits in the suffrage movement arose from a rivalry between the two most powerful groups, those in London and Manchester. When Manchester decided that all the country's suffrage groups should be banded together, they wanted the headquarters to be in Manchester (the Central Committee of the National Society for Women's Suffrage); the suffrage community in London refused to join them. Manchester also proposed that their new committee would be under the leadership of a man, Jacob Bright. He was a pioneer of women's suffrage and, as the Radical-Liberal MP for Manchester, he had the influence that no woman was yet able to enjoy. Bright was also a Quaker who believed fervently in the right of all people to be equal. Lydia Becker wrote of him in 1867, "Of [Jacob's] services to our cause, it is impossible to speak too highly. He deserves the hearty thanks of every one interested in it."[2] Despite his solid suffrage and campaigning credentials, the London suffrage groups were not keen to be ruled by Manchester and most certainly not by a man.

Other problems arose out of individual members' political feelings. Many suffragists assumed that the natural party for the suffrage campaigner to support was the Radical-Liberal party, but many women felt allegiance to the Conservative party. This caused friction at suffrage meetings, with women who felt very strongly on both sides calling for allegiance to their choice. Both Liberal and Conservative supporters were wooed into believing politicians' rhetoric that _their_ party would be the only one to take the subject of female suffrage seriously. In addition, there were many perspicacious women who were dubious about both parties, having witnessed disappointment from politicians of all persuasions in the fight so far.

---

2. Jacob Bright's sister, Priscilla, was also a leading suffrage campaigner and President of the Edinburgh National Women's Suffrage Society, at which Jacob appeared as a guest speaker.

The Morning Post, 16 February 1891

"We work consistently and persistently for the extension of parliamentary suffrage to women on the same lines on which they have been already admitted to the various local franchises. The experiment of extending the School Board, Municipal, and County Council suffrage to women has worked so well and with such a conspicuous absence of the ill effects which were feared by some, that the time would seem to have arrived for a similar enfranchising measure to be passed with regard to the parliamentary suffrage. In order, however, to avoid the danger that this important question may be crowded out by the many importunate claims on public attention, and thus fail to receive due consideration, a certain amount of machinery is indispensable. An office near the Houses of Parliament is required, the services of a well-qualified secretary must be permanently retained, meetings must be held, memorials prepared, information supplied, and, in a word, the usual apparatus of legitimate political agitation must be maintained. For this, money is needed, and the funds of our society are insufficient to meet the necessary expenditure.

There is reason to believe that some of our friends are not aware of the danger that the work may be seriously crippled by want of the means of carrying it on with efficiency, and we venture, therefore, to ask all those of your readers who sympathise with our object, and especially those who may be prevented from taking part in direct personal effort, to strengthen our hands by supplying, in adequate measure, the sinews of war.

Subscriptions may be sent to the secretary, Miss Helen Blackburn, or Mrs. Fawcett, as treasurer of the society, at our office, 10, Great College-street, Westminster.

Yours, Millicent Garret Fawcett, Florence Davenport-Hill, Emily Davies

These disillusioned women put forward the case that the suffrage cause should not be seen to ally itself with any one party. These types of breaches often led to discontented women leaving their original suffrage society to set up a rival group formed of women who shared the same party-political beliefs.

Over the ensuing years, there would continue to be splits within the suffrage movement – as increasing numbers of women declared themselves suffragists, the number of strong personalities and differing political opinions within the movement also increased. There were also splits between those within the suffrage societies who maintained that single women should be treated differently from married women (many felt that only single women should be entitled to the vote). Breakaway parties of women set up a number of smaller groups, including the WFL (Women's Franchise League), the Women's Emancipation Union, the Cooperative Women's Guild, the Women's Liberal Federation (allied to the Liberal party) and the Primrose League (allied to the Conservative Party). It was not until 1897 that a more unified suffrage movement would emerge, under the umbrella of the National Union of Women's Suffrage Societies (the NUWSS). It was founded and led by Mrs Millicent Garrett Fawcett (younger sister of Elizabeth Garrett Anderson and now married to the Liberal MP Henry Fawcett).

The history of British women's suffrage in the second half of the 19th century was not all about division, however. Although the most forceful personalities tended to be those in the most prominent positions and therefore those whose activities were most likely to be written about, the majority of women who volunteered their time, expertise or money to the cause of female suffrage worked in harmony alongside their fellow suffrage campaigners, and many real and lasting friendships were forged on the march towards the vote. Many of these mid-Victorian campaigners would not live long enough to see their hard work come to fruition, but their dedication to the cause helped to secure a more egalitarian future for their female descendants.

In 1871, Newnham College was founded in Cambridge, a huge step forward in the cause of female education – although this was still not what could be considered equality. Cambridge University might

A portrait of
Mary Wollstonecraft
(1759–1797), English
teacher, writer and
feminist. She was the
mother of Mary Shelley,
who was famous for her
novel *Frankenstein*, which
was published in 1818.

The English politician
Henry Hunt (1773–1835),
depicted in watercolours
by Adam Buck.

Caroline Elizabeth Sarah Norton *née* Sheridan (1808–77) was a writer of poetry, novels and songs, who married George Norton in 1827. As a result of her unhappy marriage, she supplied evidence leading to the passage of the Infant Custody Act 1839 and the Marriage and Divorce Act 1857.

English nursing reformer Florence Nightingale (1820–1910), is shown here in 1845. She became the first woman to receive the Order of Merit for her tireless efforts during the Crimean War.

Princess Louise (1848–1939), was the fourth daughter of Queen Victoria. She married John Campbell, 9th Duke of Argyll in 1871.

Shown here in c. 1868, George Eliot was the pen name of Marian Evans (1819–80), the novelist.

Miss Frances Power Cobbe, writer and reformer who wrote tirelessly to expose injustices against women and children during the 1870s.

Regina Cordium or the *Queen of Hearts*, 1860 (pastel on paper) by Dante
Charles Gabriel Rossetti (1828–82).
His wedding portrait was made soon after Rossetti's marriage to Lizzie
Siddal in May 1860. Her full name was Elizabeth Eleanor Siddal (1829–
62).

Amelia Bloomer (1818–94) was an American feminist and a champion of dress reform. The style of dress for women that she designed and wore was given the name of bloomers, which eventually became the term used to describe women's nether garments. Wood engraving, London, 1869.

An engraving showing a group of women in types of "Rational Dress", shown at the Exhibition of Hygienic Costume, 1882. In the 1880s, the "Dress Reform Movement" and the "Rational Dress Society" attempted to free women from the constraints and impracticalities of corsets and other cumbersome clothing.

have admitted female students, but it – in common with all the other universities in Britain – still did not permit those students to attain the same degrees as their male peers. That would not happen until 1948[3]. In 1872, when the London School of Medicine for Women was opened, Elizabeth Garrett Anderson was able to witness at first hand the power of her campaigning zeal and of her sheer determination never to give up. This inspired other women who had followed the doctor's cause and cheered at this evidence of female equality in the medical world. It was also a time for female patients to rejoice: the thought that they could be examined medically by another woman, instead of by a man, was a huge relief for many women.

The following year, another pivotal political bill was passed. The Custody of Infants Act 1873 gave all married women who were legally separated or divorced from their husbands the right to see their children, regardless of whether or not they possessed a "blemished character". The act brought about important changes to the 1839 act for which Caroline Norton (who was now in her late sixties) had fought so hard. By 1873, it had been decided that courts should make decisions about parental custody based not on the needs or desires of the parents but on the needs of the child. Under the new act, mothers were finally permitted to apply for custody of, or access to, children below the age of 16. It was by no means certain that they would be successful, but courts no longer granted custody of a child to its father automatically.

Throughout this time, Richard Pankhurst, and others, had been attempting to bring about changes to the 1857 Divorce and Matrimonial Causes Act, and in 1878 a new Matrimonial Causes Act was passed. One of its most important changes was that the new act allowed women in violent marriages to apply for a "protection order" from a magistrates' court. Unlike the earlier act, which was mostly of benefit to women

---

3. Cambridge first awarded degrees to women in 1948, but in fact the Unviersity of London was the first British university to do so, beginning in 1878.

of the upper classes, this new law was a vitally important step forward for working-class women – a protection order was far less costly and came into effect far more quickly than a divorce and, although it was not a divorce, it was in essence a legal separation, permitting a woman independent status in the eyes of the law. The new act was largely inspired by the work of the investigative journalist and campaigner Frances Power Cobbe and her pivotal article "Wife Torture in England".

Sunderland Daily Echo and Shipping Gazette, 13 August 1878

At the Clerkenwell Police court yesterday, Patrick Coolan, 52, labourer, was charged with assaulting his wife Ann. The particulars of the case showed disgraceful and systematic violence to have been used by defendant for a period of 20 years, and the unfortunate wife's face was now a mass of discolouration. Mr Hosack said this was a case to which the Matrimonial Causes Act applied. Defendant would be imprisoned for three months, after which time a grant of separation would be made, and the prisoner ordered to pay 5s per week towards his wife's maintenance.

Cobbe, who grew up in Ireland and travelled widely before settling in England, had been writing hard-hitting articles for many years, working tirelessly to expose injustices, especially those perpetrated against women and children.[4] Her article, published in

---

4. In the 1870s, Frances Power Cobbe would also turn her attention towards animals and was one of the most influential of the early anti-vivisection lobby. She founded the Society for the Protection of Animals Liable to Vivisection (which would later become the British Union for the Abolition of Vivisection or BUAV) in 1875, worked closely with the RSPCA and was instrumental in bringing about the 1876 Cruelty to Animals Act.

The *Contemporary Review*, April 1878, included the comments:

> *"What are the immediate incitements to the men to maltreat the women? They are of two kinds, I think – general and particular. First, the whole relation between the sexes in the class we are considering is very little better than one of master and slave.... To a certain extent this marital tyranny among the lower classes is beyond the reach of law, and can only be remedied by the slow elevation and civilization of both sexes. But it is also in an appreciable degree, I am convinced, enhanced by the law even as it now stands, and was still more so by the law as it stood before the Married Women's Property Act put a stop to the chartered robbery by husbands of their wives' earnings. At the present time, though things are improving year by year, thanks to the generous and far-seeing statesmen who are contending for justice to women inside and out of the House of Commons, the position of a woman before the law as wife, mother, and citizen, remains so much below that of a man as husband, father, and citizen, that it is a matter of course that she must be regarded by him as an inferior ... the political disabilities under which the whole sex still labours, though apparently a light burden on the higher and happier ranks, presses down more and more heavily through the lower strata of society in growing deconsideration [sic] and contempt, unrelieved (as it is at higher levels) by other influences on opinion. Finally at the lowest grade of all it exposes women to an order of insults and wrongs which are never inflicted by equals upon an equal, and can only be paralleled by the oppressions of a dominant caste or race over their helots.... The general deprecation of women as a sex is bad enough, but in the matter we*

are considering, the special deprecation of wives is more directly responsible for the outrages they endure. The notion that a man's wife is his PROPERTY, in the sense in which a horse is his property (descended to us rather through the Roman law than through the customs of our Teuton ancestors), is the fatal root of incalculable evil and misery. Every brutal-minded man, and many a man who in other relations of life is not brutal, entertains more or less vaguely the notion that his wife is his thing, and is ready to ask with indignation (as we read again and again in the police reports), of any one who interferes with his treatment of her, 'May I not do what I will with my own?' It is even sometimes pleaded on behalf of poor men, that they possess nothing else but their wives, and that, consequently, it seems doubly hard to meddle with the exercise of their power in that narrow sphere!"

In her autobiography, Cobbe commented, "The part of my work for women … to which I look back with most satisfaction was that in which I laboured to obtain protections for unhappy wives, beaten, mangled, mutilated and trampled on by brutal husbands."

Four years later, the Second Married Women's Property Act (of 1882) was passed. Once again it was drafted by Richard Pankhurst, who had, a few years earlier, married a young woman named Emmeline Goulden, who was as passionate about women's suffrage as he was. Thanks to Richard Pankhurst's campaigning legal work, from 1882 onwards married women were entitled to "administer their own property" and, crucially, they were allowed to retain ownership and control of any property they brought into a marriage. Many men were bitterly opposed to what seemed, in essence, the end of the lucrative dowry a man could previously have expected upon marriage to the daughter of a rich man.

At the start of 1884, there was great excitement within the walls of women's meeting rooms. The party currently in government was the Liberals, headed by the controversial Prime Minister William Gladstone (often hampered in his career by Queen Victoria's intense dislike of him). The suffragists had been informed that the Liberals were intending to introduce a new Reform Bill, which included a clause about women's suffrage, albeit a watered-down version of what the campaigners had hoped for. They were aware, however, that any change in the law would be the starting point they needed, the "thin edge of the wedge" that could lead to much greater and more wide-reaching changes – as evidenced by the great strides forward that had been made in subsequent amendments to the first Custody of Infants, Matrimonial Causes and Married Women's Property Acts. One quality that suffrage campaigners had been forced to learn and to cultivate was patience – but they remained confident that, by the end of the 19th century, women in Britain would have gained the vote. In 1884, it really seemed that the moment was about to arrive; that, thanks to the new Reform Bill, some women would attain suffrage.

When the bill was read in the House of Commons in July 1884, women all over Britain waited eagerly to hear the result. Their expectations were dashed by the news that the bill had been rejected by 271 against, compared to just 135 in favour. It was soon discovered that Prime Minister Gladstone, whom many of the women had believed was on their side, had himself spoken against the bill and persuaded many Liberal MPs to vote against it. The reason for this was that he believed that the only women who would be eligible to vote if this particular bill were passed would be those in such an elevated social position that they would almost certainly vote Conservative. The Reform Bill would therefore not benefit the Liberals, so it needed to be rewritten. This was done but, instead of being rewritten to include a wider percentage of the female population as the intended new electorate, it was amended to exclude women voters entirely. Once again, the issue of women's suffrage had been written out. When the amended version of the bill was heard at the end of the year, it was passed – entitling many more men to vote than had been allowed previously.

Frances Power Cobbe had commented on what many saw as a ludicrous imbalance between those with and those without the vote: "women [voters] ... are needed to restore the just balance in favour of an educated constituency against the weight of the illiterate male voters now entrusted with the suffrage." Before 1832, only 3 per cent of the male population of Britain had been entitled to vote; by 1885 approximately 60 per cent of men in Britain had gained the vote. Despite years of campaigning, not a single British woman was yet enfranchised.

Ironically, the official name of what was usually referred to as the "Third Reform Bill" was The Representation of the People Act 1884. Despite claiming to represent the people, the Liberals, who had promised so much to women's suffrage campaigners, had backed out of their initial promises. Their new act ignored half of the population it claimed to "represent". As Ray Strachey would later comment, "party loyalty was stronger than promises to non-voters".

There was, however, a vital piece of legislation introduced in the year of the patriarchal reform bill. The new Married Women's Property Act of 1884 declared that a woman was no longer a "chattel" (or possession) of her husband. British women may have been denied the vote, but at least they were finally declared in law "a separate and independent person" from their husband. In *The Cause*, Ray Strachey claims that even at this time women were still not fully protected, and relates the following story, which she felt brought wives' emancipation from the cruelty of husbands finally to fruition:

"It was not until 1891 that a married woman's personal freedom was finally safeguarded. In that year a Mr Jackson, whose wife had left him, obtained a decree for the restitution of conjugal rights. She refused to obey it, and one Sunday as she was leaving Church with her sister he seized upon her and with the aid of two other young men he forced her into a carriage and drove her to his house, where he imprisoned her. The wife's friends brought an action for *Habeas Corpus*, and, after long argument, and much quoting of precedents, the decision was in her favour. Henceforth a woman was a legal, as well as an actual person, free to go where she pleased, whether she was married or not."

Chapter Seven

"... It will not always be thus; the public mind is
undergoing a rapid change in its opinion of woman
and is beginning to regard her sphere, rights and
duties in altogether a different light from that which
she has been viewed in the past ages ... we feel assured
that, when a more thorough education is given to her
and she is recognized as an intelligent being capable
of self-government, and in all rights, responsibilities
and duties man's equal, we shall have a generation of
women who will blush over the ignorance and folly of
the present day."

Amelia Bloomer, in *Western Home Visitor,* 1854

It was not only in the political world that the call for female suffrage was
gaining force. Changes were being made all over the country, especially
in the worlds of fashion, healthcare, education and literature. Artists and
writers have always been on the edge of avant-garde movements, and in
the case of the "rational dress" movement in Britain (see below), the Pre-
Raphaelite, Arts & Crafts and Aesthetic artists led the field. When the Pre-
Raphaelites burst onto the scene in the late 1840s, they were considered
arrogant rebels but unlikely to prove a threat to the established order

– this seemed to be confirmed when Charles Dickens wrote a scathing article about Pre-Raphaelitism, published in his magazine *Household Words*, which not only informed the general public about this new artistic movement but also effectively warned his readers against them and their style of art. The notable art critic and writer John Ruskin rose to their defence, however, and the tide began to turn: the seven young men who had called themselves the Pre-Raphaelite Brotherhood began to move towards success. Four of the original seven – John Everett Millais, Dante Gabriel Rossetti, William Holman Hunt and Thomas Woolner – would become highly respected, very famous and very wealthy within a few years of Charles Dickens publishing his article. The Pre-Raphaelite Brotherhood grew into the Pre-Raphaelite movement, which would continue into the 20th century. Out of the movement grew several satellite artistic and literary movements, including William Morris's Arts & Crafts movement and the Aesthetic movement.

The Pre-Raphaelites are probably best known today for their paintings of beautiful women, and for their most famous models Elizabeth "Lizzie" Siddal and Jane "Janey" Morris. Both Lizzie and Janey eschewed restrictive, claustrophobic clothing, and were famously painted in loose-fitting, long-flowing dresses. Both women made their own clothes and were influential in creating a style commonly known today as Pre-Raphaelite. In their own time, this style of dressing was known as Dress Reform or the Rational Dress movement. It was spearheaded in Britain by Pre-Raphaelite models, artists and their circle, but by the 1880s it was more widely discussed and had become accepted by the literati and intellectual echelons of society – although it took many more years before it would spread throughout the ranks.

While the Pre-Raphaelites and their circle were spearheading dress reform in Britain, Amelia Bloomer was leading the movement in America. Although, contrary to popular belief, she did not invent the "bloomers" that still bear her name, Amelia was instrumental in introducing them to a wider audience, through the articles she wrote and the magazine she edited, *The Lily*. In one edition, she included a paper pattern so that readers could make for themselves the full-length, billowing trousers gathered in at the ankle, described as being akin to Turkish harem pants.

Detractors pointed out that a similar garment had been worn by women in revolutionary France and that such attire would necessarily lead to unrest and possibly violence. Undeterred by such prophecies, Amelia Bloomer famously wore her "divided skirt" under a dress that was not full-length, and thereby considered shocking, despite the fact that the bloomers covered up her legs and ankles entirely. The simple fact that her skirts did not reach down to the ground was extremely controversial.

The Pall Mall Gazette, Tuesday 11 November 1884

If, however, the divided skirt is to be of any positive value, it must give up all idea of "being identical in appearance with an ordinary skirt." It must diminish the moderate width of each of its divisions, and sacrifice its foolish frills and flounces; the moment it imitates a dress it is lost; but let it visibly announce itself as what it actually is, and it will go far towards solving a real difficulty. I feel sure that there will be found many graceful and charming girls ready to adopt a costume founded on these principles, in spite of Mr. Wentworth Huyshe's terrible threat that he will not propose to them as long as they wear it, for all charges of a want of womanly characters in these forms of dress are really meaningless; every right article of apparel belongs equally to both sexes, and there is absolutely no such thing as a definitely feminine garment.

Oscar Wilde

Amelia Bloomer also published widely on women's rights and the need for men and women to be equal. In her controversial pamphlet *Golden Rules for Wives*, Amelia, who was herself happily married, wrote, in an echo of Mary Wollstonecraft, of marriage being a form of slavery:

"Master and slave! Such they make the relationship existing between husband and wife; and oh, how fearfully has woman been made to feel that he who promised at the altar to love, cherish and protect her is but a legalized master and tyrant! We deny that it is any more her duty to make her husband's happiness her study than it is his business to study her happiness. We deny that it is woman's duty to love and obey her husband, unless he prove himself worthy of her love and unless his requirements are just and reasonable. Marriage is a union of two intelligent, immortal beings in a life partnership, in which each should study the pleasure and the happiness of the other and they should mutually share the joys and bear the burdens of life."

Before Amelia Bloomer began to garner fame, another woman in America had become known for wearing trousers. She was a visiting Englishwoman, the actress Fanny Kemble, who had moved from Britain to America following her marriage to a wealthy man from Georgia. Having arrived in America, she was appalled to discover that the source of his wealth was the slaves who worked on his estates; she tried tirelessly to alleviate their plight and eventually divorced her husband because he refused to change his lifestyle. She became a heroine of the abolition movement, writing a book entitled *Journal of a Residence on a Georgian Plantation in 1838–1839*. Following the book's publication in 1863, she gave talks and readings about her abolition work in both America and Britain – but she had already become notable, from the 1840s onwards, not only for her 1840 divorce but also for wearing trousers. She did so simply because she found them more comfortable and more practical than dresses.

The idea behind Rational Dress was a protest against the clothing and shoes that restricted a woman's movement; it was similar to the protests by Chinese women in the 20th century against the practice of foot binding. In 19th-century England, women were protesting against unfeasibly high heels, which were painful and caused foot problems – as well as restricting a woman's ease of movement. They were also protesting against many seemingly "essential" items of clothing, in particular the cage crinoline, the bustle and the corset. Many doctors had been calling for an end to the corset – especially for corsets created specially for pregnant women, which boasted the ability to give a woman a waist even in their third trimester of pregnancy. Articles were published in medical journals about the damage caused to unborn foetuses and to women's internal organs by tightly laced corsets, although for years these medical concerns were ignored by the fashionable world.

In America, Amelia Bloomer was ridiculed in the national press, and in Britain, the same treatment was meted out to those who dared go against the status quo; a woman who chose to live her life in any way differently from the accepted "norm" was bullied and derided by her own society. In the late 1850s, Lizzie Siddal ended her stormy relationship with the artist Dante Rossetti and moved to her father's home county of Yorkshire, where she attended art school. The art students she met in Sheffield were very different from those she had been associating with in bohemian London and they were unprepared for this uncorseted, uncrinolined woman. For weeks Lizzie was teased and ridiculed by her classmates, making her life miserable. The teasing only ended when the class was taken on a field trip to an art exhibition. Lizzie appeared ready to catch the train with all the other students but not wearing her usual Pre-Raphaelite garb: she had dressed up in the latest Paris fashions, bought when she had lived briefly in France a couple of years previously, complete with corset, bustle and crinoline – her outfit was far more expensive and fashionable than anything any of her Yorkshire classmates could hope to own. The teasing reputedly stopped, even when Lizzie went back to her uncorseted reformed dress, having cowed her classmates into accepting her – but it is unlikely the whisperings stopped entirely, and she did not appear ever to have been welcomed into the student group. Rational Dress was still considered shocking and unseemly.

By the time of the Aesthetic movement, the problems that Lizzie Siddal encountered were no longer such an issue. It had become extremely fashionable for both men and women from intellectual families to wear Rational Dress, as can be seen in portraits painted by artists allied with the Aesthetic movement, including G. F. Watts, Valentine Prinsep and Frederic, Lord Leighton. These depict women wearing far less "sculpted" dresses, allowing freedom of movement, whilst still preserving modesty. By the late 1870s, the most Aesthetic shop in the country was the newly opened Liberty in central London. Liberty sold a variety of Rational Dress styles, often made using their own fabrics, known as "Liberty print". Oscar Wilde, one of the most famous exponents of the Aesthetic movement, commented that, "Liberty is the chosen resort of the artistic shopper." Dress Reform had become the most fashionable style of dress in bohemian – if not mainstream – society.

In 1881, the Rational Dress Society was founded in London. It declared its beliefs in a manifesto:

> *"The Rational Dress Society protests against the introduction of any fashion in dress that either deforms the figure, impedes the movements of the body, or in any way tends to injure the health. It protests against the wearing of tightly-fitting corsets; of high-heeled shoes; of heavily-weighted skirts, as rendering healthy exercise almost impossible; and of all tie down cloaks or other garments impeding on the movements of the arms. It protests against crinolines or crinolettes of any kind as ugly and deforming ... [and] requires all to be dressed healthily, comfortably, and beautifully, to seek what conduces to birth, comfort and beauty in our dress as a duty to ourselves and each other."*

In Germany, Dr Gustav Jaeger[1] was writing about the dangers of tight, restrictive clothing and materials, and advocating the use of wool as the only fabric suitable to wear next to the skin. This negated the need in winter for layers of heavy petticoats as the wool was warm enough not to require them. Many of Jaeger's ideas began to be discussed in London, both in the medical community and in the artistic world. The Irish writer George Bernard Shaw was one of Jaeger's most ardent followers and one of the first men in London to appear in public in Rational Dress. Oscar Wilde also wrote articles about the women's Rational Dress movement – praising both Liberty and Jaeger – published during his editorship of *The Woman's World* in the late 1880s. He suggested that, although high heels were essential under long skirts for women to keep their hemlines above the filthy streets (without revealing their forbidden ankles), women should wear shoes with a built-up platform sole, rather than simply with high heels. These would help keep long skirts out of the mud without forcing the foot into an unnatural and painful shape. He also declared that dresses should be made to hang from the shoulders, not gathered in and then hanging from the hips, which is what gave rise to requirements for corsets and unnaturally accentuated tiny waists:

> *"Now, it is quite true that as long as the lower garments are suspended from the hips a corset is an absolute necessity; the mistake lies in not suspending all apparel from the shoulders. In the latter case a corset becomes useless, the body is left free and unconfined for respiration and motion, there is more health, and consequently more beauty. Indeed all the most ungainly and uncomfortable articles of dress that fashion has ever in her folly prescribed, not the tight corset merely, but the farthingale, the vertugadin, the hoop, the crinoline, and that modern monstrosity the*

---

1. The Jaeger fashion label grew out of Dr Jaeger's principles and ideas.

so-called 'dress improver' also, all of them have owed their origin to the same error, the error of not seeing that it is from the shoulders, and from the shoulders only, that all garments should be hung."

Wilde went on to praise what was being called the "Greek" style of dressing, espoused by the famous Aesthetic architect and designer E. W. Godwin:[2]

"One of the chief faults of modern dress is that it is composed of far too many articles of clothing, most of which are of the wrong substance; but over a substratum of pure wool, such as is supplied by Dr Jaeger under the modern German system, some modification of Greek costume is perfectly applicable to our climate, our country and our century.... I am sure Mr. Godwin would agree with me ... that the principles, the laws of Greek dress may be perfectly realized, even in a moderately tight gown with sleeves: I mean the principle of suspending all apparel from the shoulders, and of relying for beauty of effect not on the stiff ready-made ornaments of the modern milliner – the bows where there should be no bows, and the flounces where there should be no flounces – but on the exquisite play of light and line that one gets from rich and rippling folds. I am not proposing any antiquarian revival of an ancient costume, but trying merely to point out the right laws of dress, laws which are dictated by art

2. Godwin had been the actress Ellen Terry's lover, following her unsuccessful marriage to G. F. Watts and their separation, but they were unable to marry as Watts would not grant her a divorce. Godwin and Terry had two children together, before he left her to marry an heiress.

*and not by archaeology, by science and not by fashion;
and just as the best work of art in our days is that which
combines classic grace with absolute reality, so from a
continuation of the Greek principles of beauty with the
German principles of health will come, I feel certain, the
costume of the future."*

That Rational Dress was about healthcare reform, not only about fashion reform, was borne out in an exciting new exhibition in 1884. The International Health Exhibition was held in South Kensington, in London.[3] The exhibition included lectures and demonstrations on all subjects relating to health, including exercise, medication, cooking and clothing – as well as more political concerns, such as the need for sanitation and decent sewers all over the country, and the tackling of diseases caused by poverty and malnutrition. Items for sale included E. W. Godwin's pamphlet on "Greek Dress", the seventh edition of a book entitled *Vegetarian Cooking by a Lady*, a publication explaining how to grow "out-door fruit … in a large and continuous quantity", tracts on Temperance, recipes for "convalescent cooking" and a publication by a member of the National Health Society entitled *How To Be Strong and Beautiful: Hints on Dress for Girls*. There were also tips on packing and dressing for those about to embark on journeys to India and other parts of the "colonies", and on how to stay healthy overseas.

---

3. The exhibition was held on the site of the present-day Science Museum.

Chapter Eight

"To women as mothers is given the charge of the home and the care of children.... But this difference between men and women, instead of being a reason against their disenfranchisement, seems to me to be the strongest possible reason in favour of it; we want to see the home and the domestic side of things count for more in politics and in the administration of public affairs than they do at present."

Millicent Fawcett, from "Home and Politics" (an undated speech that Fawcett delivered several times)

On a cold Saturday night in late November 1886, there was great excitement at the annual meeting of the Edinburgh National Society for Women's Suffrage. Women arrived early in order to secure a seat at the Queen Street Hall, aware that attendance would be higher than normal. Hundreds of women – and a small number of men – crowded in to hear the guest speaker, Mrs Millicent Garrett Fawcett, address the meeting. A journalist for the *Glasgow Herald* was obviously charmed by Fawcett's personality and reported her talk in a sympathetic article:

"She said it was now nearly 20 years since this movement had begun. They had constantly reiterated the simple, straightforward, and reasonable claim that those women who fulfilled the qualifications which the law demanded of the male electors should be admitted to the Parliamentary franchise, and they confessed they had great difficulty in understanding how it was that more progress had not been made. But they should take heart and remember that 20 years was but a short time in the history of a great movement.... Since she had come to Scotland she had talked with an old lady who remembered the time when no woman in the Church of Scotland had any voice in the management of Church affairs, and when there were no woman teachers even in the Sunday-schools.... Women were now doing good work in a number of important public positions, such as Poor-Law Guardians, members of School Boards, etc.... She pointed to how much had been done for the higher education of women and how little by Government.... She knew that the Married Women's Property Act would not have been passed but for the feeling that the agitation for woman suffrage was behind it."

The journalist also reported that Millicent Garrett Fawcett had commented that "women had learned self-reliance and also to rely upon one another". This heart-warming picture of sisterly harmony was not, however, representative of all women in Britain. While Fawcett was charming the crowds in Edinburgh and creating many more converts to the suffragists' cause, there were a large number of women who did not want their gender to be granted the vote. They, together with sympathetic male supporters, began the anti-suffrage movement, which would start to gain momentum by the end of the 1880s.

The last couple of decades of the 19th century were a time of agitation and discontent. It was not only suffragists who were calling for change to Britain's political and social climate. As the century headed towards its final years, people all over the country were growing increasingly insistent that their voices should be heard by those in power. In the summer of 1887, Queen Victoria celebrated her Golden Jubilee, but for the previous 26 years she had remained in mourning for her husband, taking less and less responsibility for, or interest in, the happiness of her people. Although the Golden Jubilee encouraged a resurgence in the Queen's popularity, there were still many who felt that the monarch was utterly out of touch with the needs of her subjects and that her government cared nothing for the vast number of poverty-stricken people in Victoria's Britain. Almost exactly a year after Millicent Garrett Fawcett's successful visit to Edinburgh, what began as a peaceful demonstration about the poor conditions of Britain's workers and the desperate plight of the unemployed turned into a violent clash between police and protestors.

What the police would describe as a "riot" took place on Sunday, 13 November 1887. It began as a march through London intended to culminate in an outdoor meeting at Trafalgar Square, organized by the Social Democratic Federation (SDF). Ever since it had been laid out and opened to the public, Trafalgar Square had become popular as a meeting place for political rallies and protests. Aware of the SDF's plans for the march and meeting, the government decided to act. Politicians were angered by a recent series of protests – about working conditions and lack of work – and were determined to bring them to an end. So they voted to ban public meetings in the square and ordered the police to prevent anyone involved with the protest from entering Trafalgar Square. The SDF organizers decided to go ahead with the march and to encourage people to push through to the square in order to hold the rally as planned. The result was chaos and violence.

The artist Walter Crane, who took part in the rally, was horrified by the actions of the police. He related that the violence had "all been on one side", that the police, who were greatly outnumbered, used their horses as weapons and charged at the crowd repeatedly, forcing people up "against the shutters of the shops of the Strand" and beating them with batons. Then, with the people blocked in against the shop fronts and unable to escape, the police charged their horses directly at them again. The newspapers were divided in their reports of what had taken place: some journalists praised the actions of the police, while others were aghast at the stories they were told and the scenes many reporters had witnessed for themselves. The *Pall Mall Gazette* employed emotive language in describing the death of a stonemason, William Curwen, who, it was claimed, was fatally injured when trying to rescue a friend "from the bludgeons of the police". The paper's story appeared under the headline "Funeral of Another Victim of the Police".

The police, however, felt that their actions were justified: they believed the enormous crowd to be violent, abusive and out of control, and, as such, that they were a danger to the wealthy taxpayers whom, the police felt, it was their duty to protect against the "great unwashed" (as one constable described the protesters). Exactly a week later, protestors and police returned to Trafalgar Square. There was yet another violent clash and this time it resulted in the death of Alfred Linnell, a clerk who, some later claimed, had not even been one of the protesters. He was trampled under the hooves of a police horse and died several days later from his injuries.

The artist, designer and businessman William Morris was one of the most prominent and famous Socialists in late-19th-century London. It was he who had encouraged Walter Crane to attend the march on 13 November, at which Morris had taken a prominent position. In common with Crane, he was shocked by what he described as police brutality. Morris had his own printing and publishing company and, following the death of Alfred Linnell on 20 November, he produced a pamphlet containing a song he had written entitled "A Death Song" together with his description of the day's events and the behaviour of both the crowd and the police. It was sold for one penny, all profits from which were given to benefit "Linnell's orphans". Alfred Linnell's funeral took place in mid-December 1887 – it became a protest in itself, with Radical and Socialist politicians using it as a political event. The streets along which his coffin travelled were reportedly lined by "tens of thousands" of Londoners. The newspapers also reported that his body was "enclosed in a shell and black coffin, a brass plate on the lid bearing the inscription, 'Alfred Linnell, 41, died 3rd December, 1887, from injuries inflicted by the police in Trafalgar Square'".

Similar clashes between police and protesters would become commonplace as the suffrage and other protest movements grew in strength, in numbers and in anger. Constable Henry Hamilton Fyfe gave the following report of his actions on 13 November 1887, a day that would become known as Bloody Sunday: "I enrolled myself as a special constable to defend the classes against the masses. The dockers striking for their sixpence an hour were for me the great unwashed of music-hall and pantomime songs. Wearing an armlet and wielding a baton, I paraded and patrolled and felt proud of myself."

Fyfe's report and the language he used, which was very much the language of his era, would be echoed again and again as the police were encouraged to use similar tactics to those they had employed on Bloody Sunday, now extended to be used against women agitating for the right to vote. The scenes that took place at the funeral of Alfred Linnell would be echoed in 1913, at the funeral of a suffragette who was also killed by the hooves of a terrified horse.

Chapter Nine

"The Queen is most anxious to enlist everyone who can speak or write or join in checking this mad, wicked folly of 'woman's rights' with all its attendant horrors, on which her poor feeble sex is bent, forgetting every sense of womanly feeling and propriety. Lady Amberley ought to get a <u>good whipping</u>."[1]

Queen Victoria, from a private letter to Theodore Martin, 1866

On a summer afternoon in 1888, three young women who worked at the Bryant and May match factory in the East End of London were sacked. The reason given for their dismissal was that they were accused of having told "lies" to a journalist about their working conditions. The journalist in question was the suffrage campaigner Annie Besant, who had begun her career on the *National Reformer* and had now set up her own radical publication *The Link*.[2] In June 1888, she had published

---

1. The Queen had recently learned that Viscountess Amberley had become President of the Bristol and West of England Women's Suffrage Society.

2. Annie Besant was already a controversial figure, having published two books advocating the use of birth control. When the first book was published, she and her publisher were taken to court and found guilty of publishing a work "likely to deprave or corrupt". Annie faced six months in prison, although she appealed successfully against the sentence.

an article entitled "White Slavery in London", in which she detailed the appalling conditions Bryant and May's workers were subjected to; she wrote about the dangers of inhaling phosphorus and how little regard was shown towards the women's health. She also revealed their shockingly low wages. Despite the fact that the match company had recently announced an enormous profit, its female workers were paid between four and eight shillings a week.[3] The management at Bryant and May determined to find out who had leaked the information to *The Link* and eventually discovered the names of three employees, who had been spotted speaking to an unknown woman outside the factory gates.

Following the sacking of their three colleagues, the female workers at Bryant and May decided to take action. On the afternoon of the same day that the sackings took place, around 200 women and teenage girls walked out of the factory. They marched to Annie Besant's newspaper office and told her what had happened, then asked for her help. Taking a few of the women into her office, Annie advised them to form a committee and together they decided that the workers would go on strike. The strike was joined by 1,500 women. It was an exceptionally brave move on the part of the workers, who would come to be dubbed "the match girls" by the press. Not only did they somehow have to survive without any wages, but they were also well aware that they could end up unemployed and without a reference – something which would have made it almost impossible for them to get another job. Within a few days, the strike had become national news.

Initially, Bryant and May put up a strong fight. They enlisted the help of their media friends and gave winning interviews in which they described their workers as having been happy and friendly until they had been corrupted by the scourge of Socialism – they knew that the

---

3. To explain quite how low this wage was, contrast it to the amount received by the 12-year-old Charles Dickens. When he worked at Warren's Blacking Factory in 1824, he received six shillings a week, which was soon raised to seven shillings. Six decades later many of the girls and women at Bryant and May were earning less than a child labourer whose career had begun before the Factory Acts were passed.

majority of newspaper readers would empathize with their opinion of Socialists. Initially a spokesman said that only one woman had been sacked and it had been done because she had refused to obey orders about how to fill boxes of matches. When it was admitted that three women had been sacked, the company claimed it was not because they had revealed the truth but because they had lied about conditions at the factory. Bryant and May said that their workers had been encouraged to be untruthful by a journalist who was merely seeking a sensation. Annie Besant called their bluff. She continued to cover the story of the strike in detail and also told the tale of an old grievance, an extraordinary story from six years previously. At that time, every worker at the factory had been told that a shilling would be deducted from their salary – the money was then used to pay for a statue of William Gladstone. The workers had been given no say in the matter. Although it was the management who had decided to honour the Liberal Prime Minister, they had refused to cover the costs of this whim themselves and had forced their workers to foot the bill instead.

With every article Annie Besant wrote in *The Link*, the story gained even greater prominence in the national press. Then she called upon the management of Bryant and May to sue her – if they could prove that what she had printed about conditions at the factory was wrong. She asked them publicly to go after her rather than continue to take out their anger on a group of poor, defenceless match girls. Via *The Link*, she set up a fund to keep the strikers from starving, and she and the committee organized rallies and marches in support of the striking workers, giving the money directly to the women in need. The fund received far more support than she had hoped. In an article entitled "What Can the Match Girls Do?" Annie Besant commented, "The strike … has aroused public interest to a remarkable extent." Perhaps it was because the news story made people think of Hans Christian Andersen's heart-rending story of *The Little Match Girl*, which had been told to generations of British children since its translation in 1846, or perhaps the public was angered at the arrogance exhibited by Bryant and May, but people took the plight of the modern-day match girl to their hearts.

Bryant and May tried intimidation and indignation. They threatened to move their factories out of London – even out of Britain – which would result in multiple job losses for which the strikers would be held accountable. They threatened to sack them all and bring in new workers from Scotland, who would be grateful for their jobs. The committee remained undaunted and the "Match Girls' Strike" continued.

In addition to Annie Besant, the workers had another influential ally, the radical campaigner Clementina Black. She had been concerned for some years about the conditions in which the match workers and other factory workers laboured. One of Clementina's good friends was Eleanor Marx, the daughter of Karl Marx, through whom Clementina had come to know the work of the Women's Trade Union League and had been appointed to the executive committee. Incensed by the way in which Bryant and May were treating their workers, Clementina Black encouraged a public boycott of the company's products – and people listened to her. Bryant and May had initially felt confident that the public would be on their side, but it soon became apparent that popular opinion was turning against them and the strike was in danger of seriously damaging their reputation and their profits.

Within a few weeks, Bryant and May agreed to come to terms with the women. At a meeting with the workers' committee, the company agreed to almost every one of the women's conditions, including bringing an end to any unfair "deductions" from their pay packets. They agreed that no one returning to work would be subjected to any form of intimidation and permitted the women to form a union, which the firm promised it would recognize and listen to. The first meeting of the Union of Women Match Workers[4] was held in July 1888; Clementina Black addressed the meeting and Annie Besant was made the Union's Secretary.

In the same year, two other very important events in women's history took place. Clementina Black attended a Trades Union Congress, where she secured the first successful resolution for equal pay between men

---

4. Within a few months, the name had been changed to the Matchmakers' Union – to allow men to join as well.

and women, and, in Parliament, the Local Government Act was passed. The latter permitted some women to vote in elections for county and borough councils. The path towards female suffrage was beginning to take shape.

By the end of the 1880s, despite these small steps forward, for the women who were already involved in the fight for female suffrage, the goal seemed further away than it had done at the start of the decade. So many political promises had been made, only to be broken. Both the Conservatives and the Liberals were happy to use women as volunteers for their political campaigns, but not to grant them the right to vote when those campaigns came to fruition. To add to the suffragists' frustration, they were finding themselves hampered not only by men but also by those women who opposed the idea of women being given the vote.

In 1889, an appeal against women's suffrage was signed by 104 well-known society women. They were led by the author Mrs Humphry Ward. Her publication, which was signed in the manner of a petition, was entitled "Appeal Against the Extension of the Parliamentary Franchise to Women". It was published in the magazine *The Nineteenth Century*. Among those who signed the appeal were Beatrice Potter,[5] Mrs Leslie Stephen[6] and Mrs Herbert Asquith (wife of the future Prime Minister). It seems surprising that these women, all of whom had the benefit of an expensive and expansive education, who occupied influential positions in society and were all active in the field of furthering female education, were against female suffrage. They all, however, joined the cause for a similar reason to that 3 per cent of men of the early 19th century who had been reluctant to grant any other men the vote. The women of the anti-suffrage movement were horrified at the thought that women outside of their circle, women whom they did not consider as intelligent or as perspicacious as themselves, could be enfranchised. They were equally horrified at the notion that women of the middle and

---

5. Beatrice Potter, who would become Beatrice Webb on her marriage to Sydney Webb, should not be confused with the author Beatrix Potter.

6. Mrs Leslie Stephen was the mother of Virginia Woolf and Vanessa Bell.

lower classes might be afforded power and entitlement – they knew, as the men of the 18th century had known, that if more people were given the entitlement to vote, British society would change irrevocably. They did not want that type of change; these women were contented with the privileged society over which they presided and did not intend that it should be eroded. Initially, this anti-suffrage feeling remained relatively little heard-of outside their own community – until the first decade of the 20th century, when it would begin to gain power proportionately with the "suffragette" movement. In the 1880s, however, the word "suffragette" had not yet been coined and all supporters of the women's suffrage movement were simply suffragists – militancy had not yet become a part of their battle.

Chapter Ten

"1. Because a democratic government like that of New Zealand already admits the great principle that every adult person, not convicted of crime, not suspected of lunacy, has an inherent right to a voice in the construction of laws which all must obey.

2. Because it has not yet been proved that the intelligence of women is only equal to that of children, nor that their social status is on a par with that of lunatics or convicts...."

Leaflet, *10 Reasons Why Women Should Have the Vote,* 1888[1]

While the struggle for women's suffrage was making slow progress in Britain, on the other side of the globe, a British colony (albeit a self-governing one) was about to lead the world in introducing universal adult suffrage. Even there, it was a hard-fought battle.

Through the early months of 1893, a home in Christchurch, New Zealand, was the centre of one of the world's most important

---

1. This leaflet was produced by the Women's Christian Temperance Union and distributed to New Zealand's MPs.

suffrage campaigns. Activist Kate Sheppard, together with a tireless network of volunteers, had circulated thousands of petition sheets throughout the North and South Islands, amassing an enormous number of signatures. She had done the same the previous year, but the resulting petition from that campaign had been ignored. This year she was determined that she and her fellow workers would garner many more names and create a document the government could not ignore.

Although many in New Zealand were in favour of women's suffrage, there were also many fierce opponents of the country's women attaining the vote. The most vociferous – and most universally despised – was Henry Smith Fish, the MP for Dunedin. He had invested a great deal of money and energy into hiring people to canvass on behalf of the anti-suffrage campaign; his goal was to produce a petition with even more names on it than those the suffragists could produce.

Fish may have appeared a formidable opponent, but his plan came to nothing when it was revealed that not only had his canvassers faked many of the names on the resulting petition, but that some had been obtained under false pretences from people who had not been told the truth about what they were signing. His disgrace was a welcome respite for the suffragist campaigners. In 1892, Marion Hatton, the President of the Dunedin branch of the Women's Franchise League, gave a speech entitled "What a Difference Between a Fish and a Woman" in which she scorned the MP for his underhand methods and "false statements". Her speech included the words:

> " 'If a woman said she would,
> She would, you may depend on't;
> But if she said she wouldn't,
> Then she wouldn't, and there'd be an end on't.'
>
> And I believe there is just one matter on which Mr Fish and the women of Dunedin are quite agreed (and only one), that is, when we women of Dunedin do get

the franchise, there will be an end of Mr Fish, and he knows it!

We declare, from the personal expression of every canvasser we have out (every one of them women, good and true) … the majority of women desiring the power to vote has been most overwhelmingly large, while those who are opposed are a most insignificant minority."

One of the most important female suffrage campaigners in the Maori community was Meri Te Tai Mangakahia. In May of 1893, she addressed a gathering of Maori politicians and requested that not only should Maori women be given the vote, but they should also be eligible to sit in Maori Parliament – something the non-Maori New Zealand suffragists had not yet dared to suggest. The speech Meri Te Tai Mangakahia delivered, which recommended petitioning Queen Victoria directly, was recorded. In translation, it contains the words:

"Following are my reasons … [why] women may receive the vote and become Members of Parliament:

1. There are many women who have been widowed and own a great deal of land.

2. There are many women whose fathers have died and who have no brothers.

3. There are many women who have a good knowledge of land management that their husbands do not possess.

4. There are many women whose fathers are now elderly, and those women are very knowledgeable about the land and how to manage it.

5. Many male politicians have petitioned the Queen about issues that concern us all – men and women – yet we have still not been adequately compensated despite their attempts…. Perhaps the Queen may listen to those petitions if they are presented instead by her Maori sisters, since she is a woman too."

All over New Zealand, the suffragists continued to work tirelessly. Every day dozens of envelopes containing sheets of signatures were sent back to Christchurch. The "monster petition", as Kate Sheppard nicknamed it, was signed by over 30,000 people.[2] As each filled sheet was sent back to her, Kate Sheppard pasted it neatly to the one before, until she had an enormously long strip of paper. This she curled carefully around an old wooden broom handle, giving it the appearance and *gravitas* of an ancient scroll.

One of New Zealand's most prominent supporters of women's suffrage was the MP John Hall, and it was his task to deliver the petition to Parliament House in Wellington. Aware that this was a time history would remember, Hall chose his moment carefully. When the room was full and he had everyone's attention, he stood in the central aisle of the debating chamber and, with all eyes upon him, unfurled the scroll: holding on to the loose end, he hurled the rest of the petition away from him, watching it fly through the air and unravel as it went, the wooden core eventually coming to rest against the far wall with an echoing thud. Even in their absence, Kate Sheppard and the women of New Zealand had won their battle.

---

2. The original petition sheets bore 23,853 signatures, but before presenting it to Parliament the volunteers worked hard to add an extra 7,000 names – they had determined to reach 30,000 in order to be taken seriously by the government.

3. In 1993, New Zealand celebrated the centenary of women's suffrage. A species of white camellia, named "Kate Sheppard", was planted in the Parliament gardens and a bust of Sheppard was unveiled inside Parliament House.

On 19 September 1893, the Earl of Glasgow, who was the current Governor General, signed the Electoral Bill granting the women of New Zealand the right to vote.[3] The country was the world's first "self-governing nation" to make women full citizens. Although in earlier decades men with European ancestry had been given full voting rights before Maori men, when it came to women's suffrage, European and Maori women were enfranchised at the same time. It had been a long battle and, like their sisters in Britain, female New Zealanders had suffered several setbacks and refusals, but at last they were enfranchised. Ironically, it would take several decades before the battle would be won in the country that many New Zealanders still called "home".

While women in New Zealand were celebrating their victory – and no doubt Henry Smith Fish was keeping as low a profile as possible – on the other side of the world the 1890s would prove a deeply frustrating decade for the suffragists in Britain. The energy and excitement of the 1880s, when women truly had believed the age of equality was about to dawn, had been crushed utterly beneath the heels of both the Conservative and the Liberal parties.

At the start of the decade, Clementina Black, still enjoying the success of her work with the unions and Bryant and May, decided to tackle another contentious issue. This time, she struck at the very heart of British family life. In 1890, she published a pamphlet entitled "On Marriage", which appeared in the April edition of the *Fortnightly Review*. Her comments caused an outcry. When the author wrote that increasing numbers of British women were preferring not to marry and detailed the reasons why, she was perceived as an unnatural harpy, attempting to destroy Victorian society. She recommended that if a woman knew she was not marrying for the right reasons, she should refuse to go ahead with the wedding, commenting, "Surely, at the worst, the broken courtship will cause less pain than the unhappy marriage."

When Black explained why she believed modern women were refusing to submit to marriage, she was exposing the unpalatable fact that not every person in Britain lived in an orderly, happy, love-filled and protective home environment. She expounded the realities of why, under the current legal system, marriage was good for men but bad for women. She advocated that divorce should be more easily available and described the institute of marriage as being "transitional", since a great change – or transition – was currently taking place among modern-thinking young women. She did qualify her comments by declaring that a happy, equal marriage was far preferable to a divorce, but her critics ignored this, focusing solely on what they perceived as her scandalous comments. "At present," she explained, "the strict letter of the law denies to a married woman the freedom of action which more and more women are coming to regard not only as their just but also as their dearest treasure; and this naturally causes a certain unwillingness on the part of the thoughtful women to marry." She criticized the law-makers for being so slow to follow the spirit of the age, holding them accountable for the problems in society: "The main tendency of our age is towards greater freedom and equality," she wrote, concluding that laws were refusing to move with the times.

Even at the end of the 19th century, Queen Victoria's England remained a harsh climate for anyone living in, or in danger of, poverty, and many of those women who fought for suffrage also sought to make Britain a more compassionate society. A year after Clementina Black published her controversial pamphlet, an idealistic young woman from a wealthy family decided to leave her comfortable home in the pretty seaside town of Weston-super-Mare and move to London, where she would work in some of the city's most poverty-stricken areas. Emmeline Pethick, who would go on to become one of the most famous names in the suffrage movement, began her social work with the Sisterhood of the West London Mission. Together with her fellow missionary Mary Neal, she began working to help rescue and rehabilitate prostitutes from abusive situations.[4] There were also changes in the offing for men, many of whom, despite their own enfranchisement, still felt unrepresented by the governing parties. In the early 1890s, a new political party was

---

4. Many years later, under her married name of Emmeline Pethick-Lawrence, she would write a book about her experiences entitled *My Part in a Changing World*.

founded in Britain. For some time, there had been discussion of the need for a party to represent "working men" and in January 1893 the Independent Labour Party came into being, led by Scottish politician Keir Hardie (who had been elected MP for the London borough of West Ham North, in 1892, as an "Independent Labour candidate", having been reluctant to ally himself to either of the existing main political parties). This exciting new era in male politics, however, did little to cheer the mood of the women's suffrage campaigners. By the mid-1890s, over half a million women in Britain were eligible to vote in local elections, yet the issue of full suffrage for women – and the possibility of voting on the serious political issues – seemed further away than it had done for many years. Even the bright new political party seemed to be concerning itself solely with the needs of the male electorate.

The year after women in New Zealand attained the vote, non-Aboriginal women in South Australia were also granted full suffrage (although it would be some years before the rest of Australia followed suit). For the first 18 months, this new ruling remained just a tantalizing promise as no election was yet in sight. The historic day came on 25 April 1896 and the women of South Australia proudly took their place at the polling stations alongside men. The papers reported that 66.3 per cent of eligible men voted in the election, while amongst women the turnout was very slightly higher at 66.4 per cent. The names of many of the women who voted were printed in the newspapers, as a celebratory roll call. *The Adelaide Observer* (2 May 1896) printed a long account of the election day, including a hilariously patronizing poem:

> *"Women were everywhere, and their presence in the streets, and leavening the lumps of humanity in the crowded polling-places, no doubt had a refining influence. Never have we had a more decorous gathering together of the multitude than that which distinguished the first exercise of the female franchise ... and rarely since the days of open voting has there been so much excitement, albeit well under control. The charming spectacle of –*

'Lovely woman, hesitating
Round the booths in sweet dismay
Her gentle bosom palpitating
Lest she cast her vote away'

was presented throughout the livelong day, but it would
be a base libel upon a sex whose instinct is less liable to
err than man's reason to assert that the women failed to
realise their responsibilities – quite the contrary; they did
themselves infinite credit, displaying a level-headedness
and self-possession that called for admiration."

The journalist was particularly impressed to be able to report that, "Even the nuns exercised their franchise."[5] There was much discussion amongst women in Britain as to how it was that women in British "colonies" were entitled to vote whereas they were still being left in the political Dark Ages.

In the same year in which women in New Zealand were granted the vote, George Gissing's novel *The Odd Women* was published in England. Its title derived from a statistic commonly quoted at the time – that there were more women than men in Britain, meaning there would never be enough men to marry all the available women. Gissing's novel focused on those women whom society deemed "superfluous". The imbalance in numbers between men and women was something hotly debated whenever the question of female suffrage was raised: if all men and women were to be

---

5. Each state in Australia voted for the enfranchisement of women at a different time, with the final state to give women the vote being Victoria, in 1907. By 1926, women in all the Australian states were able both to vote and to stand for election – unless those women were Aboriginal. No Aboriginal Australian, male or female, was given the right to vote until 1962.

given the vote, then men would be outnumbered at the polling booth.

The dark decade of the 1890s made it apparent that if women in Britain were going to be able to win the vote, they would have to heal any differences between them that were damaging the campaign and work together in a much more cohesive and carefully managed way. Petitions were still being signed and local groups were banding together to try to have more influence, but it was all still coming to nothing. In 1897, a group of female artists signed a petition to be sent to Parliament calling for women's suffrage – these were women who worked for their living, many of whom supported themselves from their art. They had hoped that with the inclusion of some very famous and influential names – including that of Kate Perugini, little known today but very famous in her own time as the artist daughter of Charles Dickens – their voices would be heard. They were ignored, just as every other women's suffrage petition was ignored. It was apparent that things could not continue as they had been.

In the same year in which the artists signed their petition, the literary and suffrage worlds mourned the death of one of Britain's most successful female writers, the Scottish author Margaret Oliphant. Her work had given renewed impetus to the women's movement during this last decade of the 19th century. In 1890, Oliphant had caused a literary sensation with her novel *Kirsteen* (1890). The heroine of the book, Kirsteen Douglas, is in love with an impoverished man who has gone to India in the hopes of making his fortune. She promises to marry him when he returns. In his absence, she is forced to leave her native Scotland for England – running away from home after her father attempts to force her into a marriage with a man she does not love. Her father has threatened that if she refuses to marry the wealthy Laird Glendochart, he will not only disown her but may also murder her. Hiding in London, Kirsteen finds a job and begins to enjoy her independence. After learning that her lover has died in India, she refuses to marry anyone else, becoming a successful businesswoman and managing to restore the family fortunes – something her father and brother have been unable to do.

Margaret Oliphant was as much of an inspiration as her fictional heroine. She had started writing novels and short stories during adolescence and her first novel was published when she was 21. After a short marriage to an artist, which left her an impoverished widow with three children to support, she wrote tirelessly to provide an income. She needed the money not only for her own children but to support her brother's orphaned children as well. Oliphant wrote over 100 novels. Long after its author's death, *Kirsteen* remained a pivotal part of the women's movement throughout the struggle for universal suffrage.

As the century moved towards its end, all over the country suffrage societies were talking about the need for a central figurehead, a charismatic, intelligent leader who would be able to impress the men who ran the great political parties. Mrs Millicent Garrett Fawcett, already famed for her suffrage work, was unanimously chosen as their leader, and in November the inaugural meeting took place of the National Union of Women's Suffrage Societies (NUWSS). Millicent Garrett Fawcett was sworn in as the President. The Notice of Formation, an official document produced from the minutes of the first meeting, opened with the statement: "With a view to the more systematic and combined organisation of the work throughout the country, a National Union of Women's Suffrage Societies has been formed." It went on to state: "It is hoped that this Union will shortly become completely representative of every active non-party Suffrage Society in the United Kingdom."[6] What the NUWSS was calling for, at the very start of its campaign, was not votes for all women – not all men yet had the vote and the idea of enfranchising all social classes was still a little too avant-garde for some – but that women should be given the same voting entitlements as their male peers. The argument was that if a male property owner had the vote, then a female property owner should also be given the vote. The NUWSS phrased its aim as being "to obtain the parliamentary franchise on the same terms as

---

6. By 1913, almost 500 regional suffrage societies had allied themselves to the NUWSS.

it is, or may be, granted to men". It would be some time before the concept of votes for every adult in Britain would become a recognized cause.

The year after the formation of the NUWSS, women's suffrage campaigners were greatly saddened by the news of the death of one of their most important male supporters Richard Pankhurst. The bright young star of the suffrage movement had enjoyed a happy marriage to Emmeline Pankhurst (née Goulden). Emmeline had given birth to five children – three daughters and two sons – although the couple had been devastated by the loss of their eldest son in 1888, at the age of four. The Pankhurst children were all brought up with an independence of spirit and the knowledge that women were as important as men in the eyes of both their parents.

In early 1898, Richard's family were extremely concerned about his health, but in the summer he assured Emmeline that he was growing stronger. As Emmeline had been tiring herself by taking care of him, Richard suggested that she take their eldest daughter, Christabel, away on holiday to stay with friends in France. He would ably be looked after by their second daughter, Sylvia, who would also be able to take care of the younger children. At first, he really did seem to be recuperating, but the respite was short-lived and he sent an urgent telegram to Emmeline, asking her to return as he was very unwell. Emmeline took the first train she could to Paris, from where she travelled back to England. On reaching London, she boarded a train to Manchester still hopeful of her husband's recovery – until her eye caught sight of a fellow passenger's newspaper, on which she was horrified to read the news of the death of her husband.

From that time on, Emmeline Pankhurst devoted herself to her children and to campaigning. Although the two Pankhurst children who are best known today are Christabel (born 1880) and Sylvia (born 1882 and christened Estelle Sylvia), there was also another daughter Adela (born 1885) and a son Henry (born 1889). Richard Pankhurst had been one of the very first successful suffragist campaigners. His wife and daughters would continue his legacy and make the family name internationally renowned.

Dr Richard Pankhurst was mourned all over the country, but especially in Manchester, the city he and his family had made their home. The *Manchester Times* printed the following obituary and description of his funeral:

"The funeral of Dr Pankhurst took place on Saturday afternoon. The cortege started from the residence, Lorne House, Victoria Park, about 1.30, and the proceedings at this point were of the most simple description. Only a few people gathered at the gates, but deputations arrived from most of the learned societies and eminent clubs of the city, and at once passed through the grounds to the house. The many-sidedness of Dr Pankhurst's life, his great knowledge, his profession, and his politics, caused these to be very varied; and though often they appeared to be contradictory in character, their feeling of sorrow was general. The law, labour, literature, science and art, in all of which branches in life Dr Pankhurst was distinguished, had each their own representatives. The coffin was of plain oak ... borne on a Darley car, drawn by two bays. It bore a simple inscription recording the death and was covered with red and white flowers. On the way to Brooklands Cemetery the funeral party was joined by large detachments from various societies, most of them connected with the Labour party, to whom of late years Dr Pankhurst had devoted his great mental gifts.... As the open hearse passed out of the Brook-street gates of the park it was met by the members of a number of cycling clubs, chiefly associated with the Labour party. They led the way, riding slowly in front of the hearse.... The stream of the cyclists seemed unending, and it was estimated that there were over 400.... In the cemetery there was a crowd of about 2,000 people, including representatives of all branches of public life in the city....

The moment the coffin reached the grave it was lowered without religious ceremony of any kind, and for a few seconds the members of the family gazed down upon it in silence. Then Mr Fred Brocklehurst delivered an eloquent address on the character of the deceased gentleman. His deeds, said the speaker, expressed the fact that he valued truth and honesty more than aught else in the world, and that he was prepared to sacrifice himself, if need be, for the advancement of the opinions which he held to be dear. This was the judgement which posterity would pass upon him. His courageous fidelity to convictions would long remain as an example to be followed, and as an ideal to be attained."

Chapter Eleven

"To man belongs the kingdom of the head: to woman the empire of the heart ... In every pure and legitimate relation – as daughter, sister, wife, mother – woman is the direct assistant of individual man."

James McGrigor Allan, from *Woman Suffrage Wrong*, 1890

In the last year of the 19th century, the first International Congress of Women was held. It took place in London and was presided over by the President of the International Council of Women (which had organized the congress), Ishbel, Marchioness of Aberdeen. In an interview with the *Pall Mall Gazette* (17 December 1898) during the months of preparations for the conference, the Secretary commented: "The council is anxious that women in all parts of the country should realise the striking nature of such a congress, the unique opportunity it affords to the women workers of all nations to meet and compare experience, and the importance of making it a success worthy of the women of England." The congress was to bring together, if possible, women from all over the world – and it placed an emphasis on working women, not only women from the more leisured classes.

Female workers had been empowered by the Match Girls' Strike of 1888 and it was inevitable that more employers would start to fall foul of the unions. In the first year of the new century, it was the turn of the female textile workers to start petitioning for change. In their book *One Hand Tied Behind Us: The Rise of the Women's Suffrage Movement*, Jill Norris and Jill Liddington looked into how the suffrage campaign affected the working-class women in the industrial towns of Britain. As they explain: "The majority of working-class men had won the vote in the electoral reforms of 1867 and 1884, and by 1900 had begun to send their own representatives to Parliament. But working-class women had no such rights".

The textile workers' protest was not resolved for several years, but it was vitally important for the history of the industry and led directly to the formation of the Lancashire and Cheshire Women Textile and Other Workers' Representation Committee. It had taken much longer for this revolution to bring about change than the Match Girls' Strike had done, but the textile workers' campaigning had led to an important and wide-reaching change in workers' lives and for future generations.

The Pankhurst family were very aware of how much dissension and dissatisfaction there was among the working people in Manchester. While the women working in the textile industry were agitating for change, Christabel Pankhurst was being introduced to the world of what would become known as "militant suffrage". She had become friendly with two important suffrage campaigners, Esther Roper and Eva Gore-Booth, who introduced her to the North of England Society for Women's Suffrage. Christabel would talk for hours with her mother and siblings about the need for more direct action and the family started to feel highly critical of what seemed to them to be the ineffectual fight for female suffrage. Millicent Garrett Fawcett and the NUWSS were taking only ponderous steps forward; the Pankhursts were beginning to talk about a need for something much more direct.

In London, Millicent Garrett Fawcett was busy forging relationships with other suffrage societies all over the world. Ever since the International Congress of Women, friendships had arisen between suffrage campaigners in different countries. Millicent was asked to join the executive committee of the International Woman Suffrage Alliance; its president was the American suffragist Susan B. Anthony, a woman who had been directly involved in many North American equality movements. In the 1860s, Anthony, together with Elizabeth Cady Stanton, had founded the American Equal Rights Association. The slogan of the newspaper they also co-founded was "Men, their rights, and nothing more; women, their rights, and nothing less". In February 1902, the International Alliance of Women for Suffrage (which went on to become the International Woman Suffrage Alliance or IWSA) held its first convention in Washington, DC. The aim of the alliance was that women's suffrage societies from all over the world could share information and ideas – and, if possible, take "common action" to try and bring about an end to the inequality the vast majority of the world's women were forced to live with. In 1904, the IWSA held a second conference, in Berlin. Until the start of the First World War, the alliance held a conference in a different country almost every year.

The year after the IWSA was formed, the Pankhursts decided that the NUWSS needed a shake-up. In 1903, Emmeline, Christabel and Sylvia Pankhurst, together with their friend Annie Kenney, founded the Women's Social and Political Union (better known as the WSPU). Initially, it was not intended as a rival to the NUWSS, rather the Pankhursts and their followers wanted to work alongside the NUWSS but to work in a different way, a more militant way, and to make things *happen*. Emmeline, an astute organizer and businesswoman, was convinced that the model the NUWSS was following, which had been used in the anti-slavery campaigns and for earlier protest movements, was outdated and ineffectual. The WSPU was all about bold action and, to emphasize this, the union chose as its motto "Deeds not Words". The age of what would come to be known as the "suffragette" was beginning.

Another slogan that would come to be associated with the WSPU was the now-famous "Votes for Women". It became the battle cry of the militant suffragists, and within months of the group's formation it was being echoed around the country. In the collections of the British Museum in London is a defaced penny, one that was minted in 1903, the year of the WSPU's formation (although the defacing may have happened some time later). Over the relief image of King Edward VII's head has been carved the words "votes for women". It was a criminal offence to damage an image of the monarch, but whoever dared to do so did it with intent and the knowledge that this penny would be kept circulating, meaning that everyone who saw it would have been reminded of the need for change and the tenacity of the women's suffrage movement.

The WSPU's first militant action took place in 1904, when Emmeline Pankhurst disrupted a Liberal Party meeting in Manchester. The following year, Christabel and Annie Kenney were found guilty of disrupting an election rally. Once again, they were targeting the Liberal party. Christabel and Annie entered the Manchester Free Trade Hall where the rally was taking place and began demanding that the Liberals endorse Votes for Women. The two women were arrested and prosecuted. The *Manchester Courier* (21 October 1905) reported the court case:

> *"Mr Bell [the prosecuting solicitor] … said the defendants evidently went to the meeting with the firm intention of creating a disturbance. They appeared to have had a number of questions to put to the speakers, and, he was informed, that one or both of them mounted a seat in the body of the hall and yelled and shrieked to the utmost of their powers. They were persuaded to desist, but afterwards renewed the disturbance and were ejected from the hall by the attendants. Before they were removed, however, Miss Pankhurst spat in the faces of Superintendent Watson and Inspector Mather, and also struck the latter on the mouth. When they got outside the defendants went into South-street and began holding a meeting. A crowd gathered round them and the police took them into custody for obstructing the thoroughfare. On the way to the police station Miss Pankhurst said that, having assaulted a police constable, she felt quite satisfied.*

Mr Bell added that the behaviour of the defendants
was not such as was expected from ladies of education,
but 'it would be more attributable to women from the
slums'…. Miss Pankhurst addressing the Bench, argued
that her conduct was justified owing to the treatment she
had received at the hands of Sir Edward Grey and other
persons at the Free Trade Hall…. Miss Kenney said she
felt it her duty to do what she had done."

The newspaper also reported that when the magistrates left to consider the sentence, Christabel and Annie used the time to put up a banner declaring "Votes for Women" in the courtroom.

The two women were found guilty and ordered to pay fines. Both were fined 5 shillings for "the obstruction" or given the option of spending seven days in prison instead. In addition, Christabel was fined 10s 6d for the assault. Both women refused to pay and said they would prefer to go to prison, so they were transported to Strangeways Gaol. As they had hoped, their prison sentences helped to bring the WSPU a great deal of publicity. When she was released from prison, Annie Kenney attended an outdoor meeting in her honour, in Manchester's Stevenson Square. There she gave a speech in which she vented her fury about the Liberal party's treatment of women, especially the "thousands of Lancashire women" who did not have a voice. "They have not tamed us," she shouted to the crowd, "we have more fire in us than ever before." The square was filled with both female and male supporters of the WSPU, one of whom, Teresa Billington, proposed that no woman should submit to "any law" until women were given the vote. The age of lawlessness was truly underway.

Chapter Twelve

*"If a husband can maintain his wife and their children
without the wife going out to work, he ought to do so.
Apart from that, however, I am looking to the ultimate
effect on the race. It is not good for the race that women
should go out into employment, and it is not good for
the children when the mothers do so."*

Dr Thomas Macnamara, Parliamentary Secretary to the
Admiralty, in a speech at Credon Road School, Bermondsey,
London, 30 September 1908

Following the prison sentences of Christabel Pankhurst and Annie
Kenney, the press was full of the activities of militant suffragists.
In 1906 – the year in which British women were once again shamed
by their government when they learned that women in Finland had
become the first in Europe to be given the vote – the *Daily Mail* coined
a new word: to distinguish the activists of the WSPU from the more
genteel suffragists of the NUWSS, the newspaper came up with the
derogatory term "suffragette". From that moment on, the women's
suffrage movement was divided. The followers of Emmeline Pankhurst
took the *Daily Mail*'s intended insult and made it their own, wearing it
as a badge of honour and proudly declaring themselves suffragettes. The

followers of Millicent Garrett Fawcett continued to define themselves firmly as suffragists. The difference between the two was that the suffragettes believed in violent or "militant" action where necessary; the suffragists wanted to continue with non-violent protest.

As the WSPU stepped up its militant actions, the number of societies affiliating themselves to the NUWSS continued to grow and the newspapers fanned the flames of the schism between suffragists and suffragettes. The suffragettes' activities gave an extra impetus to the anti-suffrage movement, which also began building up its campaign. The most famous woman in the anti-suffrage campaign was the novelist Mary Ward, better known by the name she chose to adopt for her writing, Mrs Humphry Ward.[1] It was she who had published "An Appeal Against Women's Suffrage" in 1889, and who had been the force behind gathering together a hugely influential band of well-educated and intelligent society women to form the anti-suffrage movemen. Most of the women in the anti-suffrage movement were from the upper and upper-middle classes and they claimed that a woman's sphere should be entirely domestic. They did not want to discourage women from taking an active role in society but they insisted that role should be confined to "feminine" areas, such as helping to advise male politicians on local governing of schools and hospitals. Mrs Humphry Ward and her followers still adhered to Coventry Patmore's feminine ideal of several decades earlier, that a woman should be the "Angel in the House" and never the decision-maker in the Houses of Parliament.

In 1908, *The Queen* magazine published an article entitled "The Opponent's View" written by the anti-suffrage campaigner Mrs Frederic Harrison. Despite the fact that the movement had been against suffrage long before the advent of the suffragette, she used the lever of the public fury about militant suffrage to add weight to her comments. Her article included the arguments:

---

1. Her biographer John Sutherland claims that this use of her husband's name Humphry, rather than her own name Mary, was to highlight her decision to be "utterly and voluntarily her husband's property".

"We often hear of the injustice done to that small minority of women who demand the Parliamentary vote; we do not hear of the injustice done to the large majority of women who have conscientious objections to the vote, and feel that in every scheme of franchise as yet set forth a great wrong is intended to the wives and mothers of this country.... The constitutional ladies, as I may call them, for they made their demands in a constitutional way, have been swept out of sight by a number of 'irresponsibles', who have, as we think, brought discredit on the cause, and forced us into action.... though it is well that our young women should dream dreams and see visions of a happier future, it is not well that they should talk irresponsible 'rubbish' (I quote again) to poor working women.

"We have waited long for some word or sign from the constitutional suffragists to curb and restrain this flood of frothy effervescence. They have among them women of distinction well able to prick these economic and other bubbles, but no word or sign has come. So it is that the women of our league find a duty thrust upon them to speak plainly their mind, and to say openly what they think of a movement which seems to them morbid and retrograde.

"We consider that the extension of the suffrage to another sex is no simple addition to the roll of electors; it is not analogous to an extension of the male franchise. It is a vast upheaval of social institutions and habits, which must cut into the peace and well-being of families and re-act for harm on the education of children."

The most vicious propaganda put out by the anti-suffrage movement came, perhaps not surprisingly, from men, feeling under threat. The posters and leaflets produced by male graphic artists made the claims that women were physiologically and mentally unfit to make important political decisions; that women were too ruled by emotion and debilitated by menstruation and childbirth to be able to vote with a clear head; that women had far less intelligence than men and lacked basic "common sense", and that women's suffrage would lead to a neglect of husbands and children and thence to the total breakdown of society as a whole. The essence of these campaigns was the belief that if women were empowered to vote, the British Empire would never be the same again. The most unpleasant examples of anti-suffrage propaganda produced by male artists showed grotesque caricatures of women as deranged lunatics, with misshapen heads, Neanderthal-style features, unkempt hair and crazed expressions on their faces above the words "We Want the Vote". In just the same way that Nazi propaganda from the Second World War would depict Jews as untrustworthy, degenerate and frightening, the anti-suffrage propagandists attempted to make men view all women who wanted the vote as devious, insane and degenerate.

One of the most emotive arguments, put forward by both male and female anti-suffragists, hinged on the fact that the population was composed of a higher percentage of women than men. This, it was claimed, meant that women's suffrage would lead to immediate chaos. The Anti-Suffrage Society produced a leaflet entitled "Women's Suffrage – and After!" which claimed deep concern about the possibility of inequality *if* women were to be given the vote:

> *"Let it not be supposed that this agitation [by suffragettes]*
> *will be appeased by small concessions of a limited suffrage.*
> *If it be given exclusively to spinsters it will be an offence*
> *to wives and mothers who are certainly not less qualified*
> *to vote on national issues. If it be given to wives it will*
> *divide homes and leave decisions to the sex which cannot*

defend the State nor enforce obedience to the laws. If it be
extended to all adults it threatens us with a majority of
women voters."

The prospect of a voting public in which men were outnumbered by women was constantly held up as a cataclysmic disaster waiting to happen. Quite what chaos was expected to ensue was not ever outlined; it was merely enough to utter the words "a majority of women voters" to have men and some women quaking as though the end of the world was about to take place.

In London, a prominent anti-suffrage campaigner, Violet Markham, gave a speech in which she was reported to have said: "The whole sphere of Imperial legislation was entirely beyond the ken of women. It was no argument to say that there were a great number of men voters who were ignorant. Could that be any reason for flooding the electorate with an even larger number of ignorant women voters – a class whose votes were inherently more sentimental and more emotional?"

In Manchester, Mrs Arthur Somervell was reported to have been "much applauded" for her speech which included the belief that "the burden of womanhood is necessarily motherhood, which is at once [a woman's] burden and her glory". She also claimed, quite astonishingly, "The vast majority of women are against the suffrage."

That being a mother was the only importance a woman required was the society's constant message. The Anti-Suffrage Society badge showed an image of a woman sitting and reading to her children, a son and a daughter. The design suggested that the women of the anti-suffrage movement were well-balanced, well-educated and intelligent, and that women did not need the vote in order to be all those things and happy besides. The anti-suffrage movement ignored the fact that most of the famous suffrage campaigners were wives or widows and attempted to portray women who wanted the vote as embittered spinsters; much of the campaigning is vicious in its representations of single women, deriding them as "ignorant" or "stupid". In a speech delivered in Cheltenham, anti-suffragist Mrs Arthur Somervell commented:

"If it was necessary that woman's voice should be heard, and that it could only be heard through the vote, then it was necessary that it should be that of the representative women, the married women. If women represented anything as apart from men to the nation, they represented wifehood and motherhood. If they were to enfranchise single women and a certain number of widows, they would enormously add to the property vote. It was impossible that the extension of the franchise should stay at that.... Adult suffrage would hand over the sovereign power to women, and enfranchise a large number of ignorant and incompetent people.

Contemporary newspapers were full of gleeful accounts of anti-suffrage meetings, at which suffrage supporters had turned up to distribute pro-suffrage literature or to disrupt speakers in full flow. When Christabel Pankhurst was questioned, in 1908, about the anti-suffrage movement, she commented, "Every bit of opposition up to now has merely strengthened our hands, and this will probably prove a blessing in disguise.... It is not a question of argument now – the country is converted, and it is only a question of bringing pressure to bear."

Perhaps the most positive aspect of the anti-suffrage movement was the way in which it galvanized those who were pro-suffrage into joint action. The anti-suffragists' message was to prove directly responsible for the healing of many rifts within the suffrage movement, as those who were determined that women should attain equality realized that they needed to put their disparate groups' differences aside in order to strengthen the suffrage movement as a whole. In the late 1890s, a large number of new or previously dissident groups allied themselves to the main suffrage campaigning body.

Chapter Thirteen

"The taxgatherer has called upon me with singular regularity, but no official reminder has ever reached me that my opinion was desired on the subject of how those taxes were to be spent. No doubt the policeman would call with equal regularity if I transgressed the laws of the country in which I live; but no one has as yet asked for my opinion on any changes or modifications in those laws, though I could not honestly say that the interests of my sex were duly considered by the legislators who framed them."

Dora Montefiore, writing in *The Social Democrat*, 6 June 1903

A t the start of the 20th century, there was a new feeling of hope for the women's movement. The death in 1901 of Queen Victoria – a female monarch who had nevertheless shown open hostility towards the rights of other women – coincided with the start of a new century and the dawning of a new era. In 1900, Sylvia Pankhurst had admitted to a "feeling of hopelessness", yet in 1901, when King Edward VII and Queen Alexandra acceded to the throne, people all over the country felt that things were going to change for the better. The government also seemed to be more amenable when it came to listening to women. When the welfare campaigner Emily Hobhouse had arrived in war-torn South Africa at the end of 1900, she had reported back on the terrible conditions Boer women and children were suffering in British concentration camps. The War Office had finally bowed to pressure and sent out a delegation to South Africa to inspect the camps, the delegates including Millicent Garrett Fawcett. It seemed as though women's concerns and campaigns might be listened to at last.

Following the founding of the Pankhursts' WSPU in Manchester in 1903, other suffrage leaders, including Dora Montefiore, founded a new branch of the WSPU in London. Dora Montefiore was already a well-respected journalist by the time she joined the higher ranks of the WSPU. In 1903, in an article for the *The Social Democrat*, she predicted that the world order was about to change and that women had to prepare themselves for the fight:

"Social-Democracy is the next evolutionary step that has to be taken by civilised nations; everything is working towards this final casting-off by society of the rags of feudalism and the fetters of superstition.... How will women bear themselves during the ordeal? Will they prove themselves by their actions and their lives that they have thrown off slave morality, slave standards, and slave habits as the workman is doing? Will they be ready to suffer actively for what they profess to believe are their rights? Will they begin now in England by refusing, as men are doing, to pay educational rates if they, as a sex, are to lose their position on Educational Councils? Women in Scandinavia are steadily gaining rights, whilst women in England are steadily losing them. But the Scandinavian woman is a strenuous, independent creature, unspoiled by luxury, untainted by the spurious glories of 'empire'."

Dora Montefiore urged women to strive to become "economically independent, morally enfranchised, and self-respecting human being[s], whose existence has a reason, a force, and an object of its own". In the early 1900s, she led a group of suffragettes in another new protest. Although born in Britain, she had spent many years living in Australia, where she had been a leading light of the Australian women's suffrage movement. It was at her home in Sydney that the very first meeting of the Womanhood Suffrage League of New South Wales had taken place, in 1891. In the later 1890s, a few years after being widowed, she had returned to England, where she joined the suffrage movement and rapidly became recognized as a natural leader. The protest movement she helped to found was expressed by the statement "No Taxation Without Representation". Wealthy women were finally speaking out about the outrage that meant successive governments had been happy to charge tax on women's private or earned incomes, yet refused to allow those women any say in how their taxes were spent. This, the women asserted, was nothing better than robbery.

In 1905, an article appeared in the *Westminster Review* written by Elizabeth Wolstenholme Elmy, in which the author asserted that the wealthy Mrs Dora Montefiore would rather go to prison than pay taxes to a government that refused to permit her representation. The following year – the year in which Finnish women were celebrating their achievement of suffrage, leading the way in Europe – Dora Montefiore refused to pay her income tax for the third time. She had first refused to pay income tax during the Boer Wars, explaining in her autobiography, "because payment of such tax went towards financing a war in the making of which I had had no voice". During these early years of protest, goods to the value of her taxes had been seized by bailiffs and sold to provide the amount of income tax owing, but her protests had barely caused a ripple of interest outside her own community. In 1906, however, it was a different story. Together with Annie Kenney and Teresa Billington, she organized a strategy that would generate the maximum fuss – and thereby the maximum publicity – possible. "I told them that now we had the organisation of the W.S.P.U. to back me up I would, if it were thought advisable, not only refuse to pay income tax, but would shut and bar my doors and keep out the bailiff, so as to give the demonstration more publicity and thus help to educate public opinion about the fight for the political emancipation of women which was going on. They agreed that if I would do my share of passive resistance they would hold daily demonstrations outside the house as long as the bailiff was excluded and do all in their power outside to make the sacrifice I was making of value to the cause."

The newspapers took the bait, showing a keen interest and reporting with glee on what became known as "the siege of Fort Montefiore". Dora and other women of the WSPU, aided ably by Dora's maid "who was a keen suffragist", managed for several weeks to prevent the bailiff from entering Dora's house. They barricaded her riverside home, in Hammersmith, West London,[1] first against the tax collector and then against bailiffs – and women all over the country read for the first time the story of this inspiring woman's fight against the tyranny of a government that taxed women but refused to represent them adequately. The women were unable to hold out for more than a few weeks, although Dora was able to leave her home well protected by WSPU members, and still attend meetings and give a speech during the "siege".

In July 1906, the bailiff finally forced his way in and seized items from Dora's home to be sold at auction and raise the £18 the government insisted she owed. (The person who bought the items was Dora herself.) The protest had, however, done everything that the suffrage campaigners had hoped: it had brought the issue out into the public arena, making it news all over Britain. At the height of the publicity surrounding the "siege", Dora Montefiore urged other women to rise up and commit "civil disobedience in the form of tax-resistance".

---

1. Dora Montefiore's house at Upper Mall in Hammersmith was just a few doors away from Kelmscott, the house in which the artist and Socialist leader William Morris had lived.

In Dora's 1925 autobiography, she remembered the weeks during which her home became a rallying ground and barricade – and the often unexpected kindness of those who supported her throughout:

"As is well known, bailiffs are only allowed to enter through the ordinary doors. They may not climb in at a window and at certain hours they may not even attempt an entrance. These hours are from sunset to sunrise, and from sunset on Saturday evening till sunrise on Monday morning. During these hours the besieged resister to income tax can rest in peace. From the day of this simple act of closing my door against the bailiff, an extraordinary change came over the publicity department of daily and weekly journalism towards this demonstration of passive resistance on my part. The tradespeople of the neighbourhood were absolutely loyal to us besieged women, delivering their milk and bread, etc., over the rather high garden wall which divided the small front gardens of Upper Mall from the terraced roadway fronting the river. The weekly wash arrived in the same way and the postman day by day delivered very encouraging budgets of correspondence, so that practically we suffered very little inconvenience, and as we had a small garden at the back we were able to obtain fresh air.... At the evening demonstrations rows of lamps were hung along the top of the wall and against the house, the members of the W.S.P.U. speaking from the steps of the house, while I spoke from one of the upstairs windows. On the little terrace of the front garden hung during the whole time of the siege a red banner with the words painted in white, 'Women should vote for the laws they obey and the taxes they pay'."

Dora's memoirs also include descriptions of what today would be called the paparazzi, "men with notebooks, and men with cameras" who camped outside the house and crept stealthily and "furtively" around the outside walls, attempting to find an angle for their eagerly awaited stories. She was favourably impressed by the police who had been posted to guard the house and who refused to allow any of the persistent journalists to climb over the wall into her garden (all were hoping for a scoop and the chance to write that they had been "inside the siege").

Some weeks after the "siege" had come to an end, Dora Montefiore made the newspapers again. In October 1906, it was reported that 11 women had been sent to gaol following a "riot" in the lobby of the House of Commons and an ensuing scuffle with police outside Westminster Police Court. As the journalist who had written an article for several regional newspapers pompously reported – obtusely missing the point of the women's campaigning methods – Dora Montefiore and Annie Kenney were among those "women who prefer life in Holloway Prison to paying sureties for future good behaviour, or paying a small fine". Among the others arrested were the artist Irene Miller, the sisters Adela and Sylvia Pankhurst (both described simply as a "school teacher"), Emmeline Pethick-Lawrence (erroneously given the first name of "Emily"), several suffragettes whose status in life was defined only by the word "married" and "Edith How-Martyn A.R.C.S., B.Sc." who was labelled as a "secretary".

The journalist described the women in court as hysterical bestial creatures. By contrast, the magistrate was "a gentleman of kindly, benevolent appearance wearing a long, grey beard" (as though he were a benign Father Christmas), who was faced by a "wild tumult" of women "like wild animals in a cage". He reported that the suffragettes "shook their fists at [the benevolent magistrate], shouted that they did not acknowledge the authority of the Court, screamed that they would not obey it, and so struggled and resisted when the police instructed them to move away that they had to be removed forcibly". They also "giggled audibly" when being sentenced, which incensed the magistrate (and the journalist), despite his reported "mild countenance". The women all wore badges proclaiming "Votes for Women" in the courtroom and the middle-aged Dora Montefiore shocked those present by sensationally producing from inside her dress a "large red banner" which she waved defiantly.

In spite of the red banner, it was Sylvia Pankhurst who made the biggest headlines. After an eager suffragette managed to release her friends from imprisonment in a room adjoining the courtroom and to imprison in their place a police constable, the officers became incensed. As Sylvia was the most vocal and the most physical in her demonstrations, the police seized her as the ringleader and carried her – with her clothing dishevelled and her hat lost amid the mêlée – out into the street, past jeering crowds. "Finally she was dragged to the police station, a woeful-looking object," one journalist noticed. Her clothing had been torn, her hat had been trampled, "but she was not yet beaten. Not until the station door had closed upon her was her voice silenced." For that separate offence of public disorder Sylvia Pankhurst was ordered to pay 20 shillings or go to prison for 14 days. She chose prison.

Following her sentence, Emmeline Pethick-Lawrence sent a message to the women of England which read: "We go to prison for you, and therefore go gladly. Bear the standard on to victory." Her husband, Frederick Pethick-Lawrence (a politician who would later become Secretary of State for India and Burma), pledged to give money to the suffrage cause in support of his wife, publicly declaring that he would pay the WSPU "£10 a day for each day that my wife remains in prison". The couple were already notable for the equality of their marriage, having caused a stir in polite society when, instead of Emmeline Pethick forsaking her maiden name to become Emmeline Lawrence upon marriage, they chose to both use the two names together. The couple had met through Emmeline's social work in the East End of London and both of them were passionate about trying to forge societal change.

That the first public disturbance by suffragettes had taken place at a Liberal rally was no coincidence. The feeling against the Liberal government – the party so many suffragists and suffragettes had once put their faith in – was running high. The Pankhursts, Annie Kenney and their followers regularly disrupted Liberal party meetings and rallies, calling for the Liberals to back their cause and, once the party was in government, demanding to know why the politicians were refusing to honour promises they had made before they came to power. In 1905, with a general election looming, Dora Montefiore had published a short article entitled "Liberal Leaders and the Enfranchisement of Women". This was following the meeting at the Free Trade Hall after which Annie Kenney and Christabel Pankhurst had been arrested. Newspapers had helped to turn the public against the women because of what were seen as violent actions, so Montefiore explained why the political meetings were being so frequently targeted by suffrage campaigners, and why Annie and Christabel had felt forced into action:

"We have so long been kept quiet by promises from statesmen when out of office, and tricked by the same statesmen when in office, that it is not astonishing if the younger and less patient in our ranks attempt to force public answers from leaders of a party which expects confidently to be in the near future returned to power. In spite of the passing of the resolutions referred to, organs of the party, such as the Manchester Guardian, keep silence on our claims, while in their editorial columns they suggest 'manhood suffrage'. Women are growing weary and exasperated."

At the general election in January 1906, the Liberals enjoyed a landslide victory. The party won 400 seats, including several which had been considered Tory strongholds. The Conservatives, whose previous government had become extremely unpopular, won just 129 seats, while the newly emerged Labour party secured 29 seats as the Labour Representation Committee. The new Prime Minister, Henry Campbell-Bannerman, was confidently expected by those women who had worked tirelessly as volunteers for the Liberal party in the run-up to the election to bring about female suffrage; they were to be sorely disappointed. In May 1906, a delegation of women from the WSPU and NUWSS had a meeting with Campbell-Bannerman. They were dismayed by his insistence – now he was safely in power – that it was "not realistic" for suffrage campaigners to expect his government to bring about changes. This was not the message that had been passed on by Liberal MPs to their female supporters before the election. The reaction towards the party and what was perceived as broken promises was one of fury. The suffragettes vowed that they would continue to target the Liberals until women were given the vote.

In June 1906, Annie Kenney addressed a women's suffrage demonstration in East Ham, London. In her speech she proclaimed: "We are going to fight the three men who, as one of the members of the Cabinet told us, are our chief enemies. The greatest of these is Mr Asquith. He is not only an enemy of the women, he is an enemy of the workers." Herbert Henry Asquith would prove himself to be outspokenly against female suffrage. His second wife, Margot Asquith, whom he married in the 1890s, was a prominent member of the anti-suffrage campaign, notoriously deriding suffragettes as being "wombless, vicious, cruel women"; she believed that most women, including those of the working class, were intellectually inferior to herself. When Campbell-Bannerman resigned through ill health in the spring of 1908 (he would die a couple of weeks later), Asquith was appointed Prime Minister. His relationship with the suffrage campaigners did not improve, and he appeared determined to go against them at every turn. In 1909, one disillusioned former supporter commented, "We have been hewers of wood and drawers of water for the Liberal Party too long." In 1916, a WSPU poster was printed describing the politician as "THE RIGHT DIS-HONOURABLE DOUBLE-FACED ASQUITH" and announced: "The Government pose as champions of the constitution, but deny constitutional liberty to women."[2]

---

2. Part of the collection at The Women's Library in London.

Dora Montefiore later wrote, with hindsight, her opinion of what went wrong in the Liberal government: "I believe the Liberal slump set in when the leaders refused to recognise the claims of women to political representation. It was a great betrayal of Liberal women who had helped the party into power, and the party has never yet morally recovered from the effects of that betrayal."

Although the WSPU had seemed so strong and united during "the siege of Fort Montefiore", by the end of 1906 a serious rift had started to appear between its Manchester and London branches. The Pankhursts had accepted that they needed to be closer to the political action and had therefore moved their WSPU headquarters from Manchester to central London. The new office was at the home of Emmeline and Frederick Pethick-Lawrence, at Clement's Inn. Emmeline Pethick-Lawrence became the WSPU Treasurer and her husband helped with raising awareness and personally funded many of their campaigns.

As well as moving the WSPU headquarters to London, Christabel Pankhurst moved herself into the Pethick-Lawrences' home, and they lived together very companionably – at the beginning. Annie Kenney and Sylvia Pankhurst also moved to London, where they began to work with the capital's poorest communities in the East End; this would inspire Sylvia's ground-breaking social work, just as Emmeline Pethick-Lawrence had been inspired several years before. Unfortunately, the London WSPU was not big enough for the celebrity, and egos, of both Dora Montefiore and the Pankhursts, and the two soon began to clash. Many of the WSPU members were also calling for more "democracy" within the ranks, which had the opposite result: Emmeline Pankhurst decided to cancel that year's AGM, feeling she needed to take a firm hand with the rebels. At the end of 1907, several prominent suffragettes and members of the WSPU executive committee, including Teresa Billington Greig and Charlotte Despard, resigned from the WSPU and set up the Women's Freedom League, or WFL. They took with them a large percentage of the WSPU's members. In his book *The British Women's Suffrage Campaign 1866–1928*, Harold L. Smith estimates that around 20 per cent of the WSPU left to join the WFL, and that these were predominantly working-class women.

For many in Manchester, the WSPU move to London was perceived as signifying that the movement was forgetting its working-class roots. Despite the fact that Annie Kenney – a former cotton worker – was one of the most important and influential members of the WSPU, many loyal suffragettes were concerned that their leaders were now interested in achieving votes only for wealthy women. They were determined that working women all over the country should not be forgotten. At an open-air rally in Wigan, in 1906, suffragist and former millworker Selina Cooper[3] gave a rousing speech, in which she declared: "Every woman in England is longing for her political freedom in order to make the lot of the worker pleasanter and to bring labour reforms which are wanted. We do not want it as a mere plaything."

In recent decades, history has muted the voices of many of the women who fought so valiantly for recognition and equal rights. The history of the women's movement has been overwhelmed by recollections of the forceful Pankhurst family – for many the words "suffragette" and "Pankhurst" are synonymous – but while the Pankhursts were an incredibly charismatic force in the suffragette movement, and Millicent Garrett Fawcett was a tower of strength for the suffragists, there were many thousands of women who fought alongside them. Had it not been for this army of women – and men – who spent all their spare time composing letters, handing out leaflets, attending the marches and swelling the ranks at rallies, Fawcett, the Pankhursts and the few other "famous" suffragettes and suffragists would never have been able to achieve what they did.

One of the defining books about the women's movement is *One Hand Tied Behind Us*, by Jill Liddington and Jill Norris, for which

---

3. Selina Cooper was the daughter of a railway labourer and a dressmaker. Following the death of her father, she started part-time work while still at school, and worked in factories, as a nurse and as a social campaigner. She and her husband were committed Socialists and worked tirelessly at a number of political campaigns. She was a loyal member of the NUWSS and in the 1920s stood as a Labour candidate in local elections (but was not elected).

the authors painstakingly tracked down those "forgotten" radical suffragists, women who worked in the factories and mills and shops of the industrial north of England, and who fought the campaign while also working full-time and raising families. Too many references to the suffrage movement depict only middle- and upper-class women, forgetting how much of the hard work was done by the nation's poorest and most disenfranchised women. In her book *Votes for Women*, author and historian Dr Diane Atkinson writes that the 1890s was an era of "radical suffragists – the vote had to be more than a symbol of equality; the lives of working-class women *had* to improve", and she explains how the rallying calls of the radical suffragists galvanized factory workers all over Britain to join their local suffrage societies, swelling the membership dramatically.

Jill Norris and Jill Liddington's book title was taken from a poignant quotation from Hannah Mitchell, a committed campaigner for women's suffrage who knew what it was to fight for justice while working for her living, as opposed to those campaigners who had servants to work in their homes and enough money to allow them a certain amount of freedom to carry on their campaigns. "No cause can be won between dinner and tea," she wrote, "and most of us who were married had to work with one hand tied behind us."

Chapter Fourteen

"If I might illustrate my meaning from football ... both have the same goal, but the suffragettes are, perhaps, the forwards in the game, while the older suffrage societies are the backs and halves."

Mr E. Richmond, Chair of the Reigate Branch of the
Central Society for Women's Suffrage, at a meeting in Redhill,
September 1907

While the WSPU was suffering internal warfare, the NUWSS was going from strength to strength. Thanks to both the NUWSS's and the WSPU's publicity campaigns, increasing numbers of women were finding out about the suffrage movement and, with the start of a new century and a new era of monarchy, many women felt less stifled than they had under the elongated reign of Queen Victoria. During the first decade of the 20th century, the number of regional branches of the NUWSS more than doubled, and in the 1910s, they increased tremendously. In her book *Votes for Women*, Dr Paula Bartlett states that the number of NUWSS branches around Britain grew from 33 in 1907 to 478 in 1914.

The relationship between the leaders of the WSPU and the NUWSS was friendly, as they realized that they could work side by side (although many of the two groups' members did not agree with this sentiment). Both the Pankhursts and the Fawcett faction had positive words to say about each other's campaigns, and when the first 10 WSPU members were sent to Holloway Prison, Millicent Garrett Fawcett went to the prison to report back on the conditions in which they were being kept. On 11 December 1906, she held a banquet in honour of the released WSPU prisoners at the new and fashionable Savoy Hotel,[1] on the bank of the River Thames in London. The invitation to the banquet was accompanied by a statement which set out her feelings on militant suffragism:

"I need hardly say that I am convinced that the work of quiet persuasion and argument form the solid foundation on which the success of the Women's Suffrage Movement is reared; and I, in common with the great majority of suffrage workers, wish to continue the agitation on constitutional lines; yet we feel that the action of the prisoners has touched the imagination of the country in a manner which quieter methods did not succeed in doing. Many of us desire, therefore, to offer the prisoners some public mark of the value we attach to their self-sacrificing devotion."

Millicent Garrett Fawcett was often criticized – by both suffragists and anti-suffragists – for her support of the WSPU and militant

---

1. The Savoy Hotel had opened in 1889, but the latest additions, including its extremely modern and now famous American Bar, had not been finished until 1904. The Savoy was very popular with visiting Americans because, unlike most British hotels of the time, it boasted hot and cold running water in all the bedrooms. It was also a popular meeting place for artists and writers; Claude Monet had stayed at the hotel between 1899 and 1901 while he painted his famous riverscapes of the Thames.

suffragettes. Her response was always that she supported suffragettes when they were the victims of violence, but not when they were the instigators of it.

A number of pro-suffrage MPs attended the banquet, as did several celebrities, including the writers George Bernard Shaw and Israel Zangwill. Earlier that year, George Bernard Shaw had written an article in the *Tribune* in which he applauded the militant actions of the suffragettes, adding that in his opinion women should agitate for revolution: "They should shoot, kill, maim, destroy – until they are given the vote."

In November 1907, the suffragette Mrs Anne Cobden-Sanderson journeyed to the United States to give a talk at Bryn Mawr college entitled "Why I Went to Prison". She had been invited by the college's newly formed Equal Suffrage League. The first ten WSPU prisoners had become celebrities – but their insistence that they were political prisoners, not mere criminals, was something that neither the government nor the British legal system would honour.

As increasing numbers of suffrage campaigners began to follow a militant course, the government would begin to respond with increased brutality. While those in power practised violence against the campaigners, the women themselves formed a network that cared for one another in adversity. Women prisoners recalled great kindnesses shown to them by other prisoners and, at times, by wardresses. Those who had been sent to prison were comforted to know that their WSPU colleagues would ensure their families would not suffer too much while they were away. Children were often cared for by other WSPU members and the more wealthy members provided financial support for the families of poorer women prisoners to compensate for lost income while the mother, or daughter, was incarcerated. When the prisoners were released, other WSPU members would care for them until they returned to full health.

Although the WSPU prisoners were fêted in certain quarters, the vast majority of the general public was horrified by their actions. Public sensibilities were particularly outraged in 1907 by the emotive case of the "Baby Suffragette", Dora Thewlis. She was a teenage mill worker from Huddersfield who had ended up in Holloway Prison, many miles from her native Yorkshire. At the age of 16, she had travelled to London as part of a suffragette plan to enter the House of Commons and set up a "Women's Parliament" (described scathingly by newspapers as simply a plan to "break into the Houses of Parliament"). Journalists took Dora as their anti-suffrage mascot, featuring pictures of her looking dishevelled and making the most of her young age. The *Manchester Courier* reported:

> "One of the defendants was a young mill girl named Dora Thewlis, of Huddersfield, who was in shawl and clogs, and when she appeared the magistrate said she appeared to be quite a child, and she ought not to have been brought up to London and turned adrift in the streets to face the police. She ought to be at the school, and he asked her if she would go back. Miss Thewlis, a comely little lass, said she would not. She had come up to represent her mother and sisters, who could not come. Mr. Smith: You ought to be with your mother. (Laughter.) He added that the way in which these women had been brought into London was disgraceful to anybody who had any action in it. The prisoner would be remanded for a week and he would communicate with her father and mother."

A reporter for the *Evening News* in London visited Dora in prison, where it was reported she was so unhappy she told him she had only cheeked the magistrate because she wanted to be the same as the others in court and that she had "regretted it ever since". The slant of his article portrayed Dora as a repentant, wronged girl who would never be interested in suffrage again. This version of the story, which was reported in newspapers all over the country, suggested that Dora had learnt her lesson and should be pitied as a victim of the suffragette cause. After her release, the *Lancashire General Advertiser* wrote emotively:

"Miss Dora Thewlis, the young suffragette, who was released by the magistrate on Wednesday is lying seriously ill at her Huddersfield home. Her exciting experiences in London and the rigours of her prison treatment have, says a London 'Evening News' correspondent, proved too much for her. She has broken down, and her parents have been compelled to summon medical assistance. Her father and mother are indignant at what they consider their young daughter's harsh treatment in prison. They are determined that the matter shall not be allowed to rest where it is, but are arranging to bring Dora's sufferings to the notice of the Home Secretary."

The country's newspaper readers enjoyed outrage over the Baby Suffragette case, and across breakfast tables all over the country spirited conversations took place blaming the Pankhursts and their ilk for Dora's seduction to the frightening streets of London and for her subsequent career in crime. The newspapers twisted Dora's story into a modern-day morality tale, as though she were the doomed heroine in William Hogarth's *The Harlot's Progress*; yet the truth was rather different and far more radical. What the public would have liked to believe was that Dora had been chastened, had learnt her lesson and had realized she should be content with her allotted role in life. In reality, her parents were incensed by what they saw as the patronizing letter sent to them by the well-meaning magistrate, and furiously vocal about the prison service and a government that allowed such brutality. Dora's family praised her for her bravery and, despite her genuine fear of going back into prison, she did not slink away into obscurity; instead she continued to fight for suffrage and was considered a pioneer by her peers.

The "suffragette raid" in which Dora Thewlis took part had been organized in Manchester by Emmeline Pankhurst, who had appealed directly to working women to join the fight. In 1943, a resident of Derby, Mrs Ford, was interviewed for her local paper (because she had won first prize in an allotments competition). During the interview she recalled her past as a suffragette and her part in the Women's Parliament plan. She had been working in Bolton when she heard Mrs Pankhurst appeal for volunteers; she remembered that she was among 60 local women who travelled to London to take part in the assault on the House of Commons. The journalist reported her account:

> *"The day of the 'raid' arrived, and the women went into Westminster Abbey to wait for the appointed time. Mrs Ford says that, as far as she could see, nobody seemed to take any notice of them as they went into the Abbey, but when they came out a great crowd had collected and there was a double cordon of policemen.... This did not deter the women, and, led by Mrs Pankhurst ... and Sylvia, they charged towards the iron gates only to see them swing to just as they reached them. 'Mrs Pankhurst had told us to keep moving wherever we were, so that we could not be arrested for obstructing the pavement,' said Mrs Ford.... 'A policeman came up to me and said "Get off the pavement",' said Mrs Ford, 'but I told him that I had just as much right on the pavement as he had! We were all arrested.'"*

Mrs Ford was sent away by the police without going to court, and had never been told why she had been singled out and dismissed when the others were arrested. She told the interviewer that she put it down to her "looking rather delicate". She recalled that the policeman who freed her was in a bad temper and said, "I'm fed up with you women. You've kept me from my lunch all day."

Despite Millicent Garrett Fawcett's open support for the suffragettes and their militant actions, many NUWSS members were furious that the WSPU had been, as they believed, giving the women's movement a bad name. It was decided a non-militant event was needed, to remind the public at large that not all suffragists adopted the same stance as the Pankhursts and their followers. In February 1907, a large number of suffragists headed to London for what was described on the posters as a "United Procession of Women". It seems extraordinary that the organizers had opted to arrange an *outdoor* event during a London winter, but the date had been agreed for Saturday 9 February 1907 and the newly elected President, Millicent Garrett Fawcett,[2] was proudly at the helm. No suffragettes took part, because the Women's Liberal Federation (known as the WLF) refused to join the demonstration if the WSPU was invited. A snub to the WSPU's methods of campaigning was implied in the NUWSS literature about the event, which exhorted women to "TAKE PART in this Procession and prove your earnestness in a manner both effective and constitutional..." It also encouraged supporters: "URGE ALL your friends to come and by your numbers make the day memorable for ever, as one which convinced Parliament and the country that the time was ripe for your enfranchisement."

The demonstration might not have convinced Parliament, but the day was certainly memorable. The relentless rain turned the streets and parks of London into a quagmire and 9 February 1907 would be remembered by history as the day of the "Mud March". Those who took part recorded in diaries their dismay as they awoke to the sound of torrential rain. Some convinced themselves it would stop, but the morning continued grey and waterlogged. Miraculously, the rain started to ease in London by 2pm, the time the procession marched through the streets, but the conditions were still unpleasant and many women stoically faced the realization that their skirts, petticoats and

---

2. Although Elizabeth and Millicent are the most famous of the Garrett sisters remembered today, in their lifetime their sister Agnes was also very well-known. Together with their cousin Rhoda Garrett, she set up the very first female house-decorating business and became very successful, despite having to put up with initial scorn about women entering such a "masculine" business. Before her early death, in 1867, their sister Louisa was also very involved in women's suffrage. Had she lived, she would almost certainly have been marching alongside Elizabeth, and the niece who bore her name, at the head of the Black Friday march in 1910.

boots were going to take many hours to get clean again. Contemporary accounts related that 3,000 women joined the march despite the weather; it seems likely there would have been many more had the weather not made travelling from outside London so difficult.

Manchester Courier and Lancashire General Advertiser, 15 February 1907

The joint women's franchise demonstration in London on Saturday was an historic occasion. It was the largest and most successful demonstration that has yet been organised in the case, its success being all the more remarkable owing to the inclement weather, for rain had fallen almost continuously throughout the morning, and the streets were rivers of mud and slush. The demonstrators were not unrewarded, for judging by the demeanour of the crowd assembled en route, which in some parts was quite enthusiastic, the proceedings created a favourable impression on the public mind. The demonstration also differed from previous ones in the social status of the women composing it. Though a perfectly friendly understanding existed between the various women's unions represented and the "suffragettes" who have lately been so much before the public, the latter body were not officially invited to take part in the proceedings for fear of alienating a number of supporters who do not approve of their extreme methods. A number of the "suffragettes," however, attended unofficially, including Miss Pankhurst, Mrs Pethick Lawrence, Mrs Martel, Mrs Martyn, Miss Kenny, Mrs Drummond, and Mrs Cobden-Sanderson. The bulk of the women, however, who were present at Saturday's demonstration were evidently drawn from well-to-do lasses. Several ladies of title walked in the procession, including Lady Frances Balfour, Lady Strachey,

Lady Onslaw, Lady Fetch, and Lady Dorothy Howard,
while two of Lady Carlisle's daughters carried standards.
Mrs Patrick Campbell and her daughter also joined the
long procession of vehicles in their carriage… Two brass
bands furnished the music. A conspicuous feature of the
procession was a number of Manchester lads who had
accompanied their suffragist sweethearts to London. To
do the thing "in style" they chartered an electric cab, and
packed themselves inside like sardines in a box. Each
of them was supplied with the suffragist colours, and
some of them went so far in their enthusiasm as to tie
rosettes to the tops of sticks which they waved through
the windows of the cab. Having assembled in Rotten
Row, the demonstrators marched through the muddy
streeets to Trafalgar Square, where women representing
the Northern textile industries branched off and held a
meeting, which was addressed by Mr. Keir Hardie, M.P.,
who asked that those who were opposed to the movement
would treat it seriously. He hoped no working man was
going to bring discredit on the class to which he belonged
by denying to women those political rights which their
fathers had won for them.

The sight of so many women of all classes walking quite openly, unchaperoned by men, was shocking to many of the spectators, and the spectacle was derided as "unfeminine". The marchers began in London's Hyde Park and walked to Exeter Hall, which stood on the north side of the Strand and had once been the favoured meeting place of the anti-slavery movement (it was a poignant moment for many of the campaigners, as the hall was doomed to be torn down just a few months after the Mud March). Many of those who took part recorded that they were jeered at and insulted as they marched through the streets, yet despite such unpleasantness, the overall supportive atmosphere and the feeling of solidarity was one that they treasured and remembered.

Many participants braved serious displeasure from family members and, in the case of working women, anger from employers, simply for having taken part in the march, but they risked it because their cause was so important to them. Such parades would become regular occurrences over the next couple of decades, but to have attended this very first one was, for many, a daring and brave action. In years to come, having taken part in the Mud March became a badge of honour, and women proudly recalled their memories of being part of the first women's suffrage parade.

Following the Mud March, the NUWSS was back in the public eye, although its activities never made quite such sensational headlines as the WSPU's. In 1907, the NUWSS drew up a new constitution and opened new offices. In being elected President, Millicent Garrett Fawcett had beaten her friendly rival Lady Frances Balfour. The two women worked closely together and were able to rely on one another's support and encouragement over the ensuing battles for the vote. Lady Frances was President of the London Society and the sister-in-law of Arthur Balfour, former Conservative Prime Minister. (His government had become incredibly unpopular, enabling the Liberals to win such a landslide victory at the recent general election.) Because Millicent's husband, Henry Fawcett,[3] had been a Liberal MP, the election of the NUWSS President was perceived by many to be another Liberal victory over the Tories. This would become a factor in the cracks that started to show in the NUWSS's veneer over the ensuing years; the NUWSS would soon begin to suffer from similar internal vexations to those of the WSPU.

On 1 January 1913, Philippa Strachey (known as Pippa), a key figure in the NUWSS, wrote to Millicent Garrett Fawcett to thank her for a gift (of "a brown owl and an exquisite paper cutter") and commented:

"Internecine feuds are more hateful than can be said & it is a great addition to their horror to think that you are being worried about them. I do not think though, that you need ever be afraid of any really

---

3. Millicent Garrett Fawcett had been a widow since 1884.

grave scandals because we are all of us too deeply attached to the N.U. in the abstract and to the President in the concrete.

Meantime I shall hang up my Owl in the office and endeavour to emulate her wisdom and divert my attention from her delightful claws."[4]

Although the NUWSS and the WSPU are the two suffrage societies that most people hear about today, there were many other groups, often small societies forged amongst groups of workers or within local communities. The year 1907 saw the founding of the Artists' Suffrage League, as well as the Men's League for Women's Suffrage.[5] Over the next few years, multiple new societies were set up, including the Actresses' Franchise League, the Women Writers' Suffrage League, the Barmaids' Political Defence League, the Church League for Women's Suffrage, the Tax Resistance League, the Men's Political Union for Women's Enfranchisement, the Catholic Women's Suffrage Society and the United Suffragists (a group created for both men and women, something of which Christabel Pankhurst was said to disapprove).

One of the founder members of the Men's League for Women's Suffrage was Laurence Housman, a book illustrator and writer (and younger brother of A. E. Housman). The League was founded in London, but within a couple of years there were affiliated societies being set up around Britain. Laurence Housman was much more famous in his own time than he is today. He moved in avant-garde artistic and literary circles and courted controversy by writing about taboo subjects. His plays were often banned in Britain by the censorship laws, meaning that many of them premiered overseas. His writing included "The Bawling Brotherhood", a short story written in the style of a fairy-tale

---

4. This letter can be seen in the collection at the Women's Library in London.

5. 1907 was also the year in which the Eugenics Education Society was founded, a movement that sought to prevent "unfit" people having children. "Only *healthy* seed must be sown! Check the seeds of hereditary disease and unfitness by eugenics," proclaimed its literature.

for adults about a land in which women had the vote and men were agitating for it. It included the words: "the main reason given by the opponents for men not being granted the vote was that they could not be mothers of children; and as they could not risk their lives in giving citizens to the State, they must necessarily be regarded and treated as 'the irresponsible sex'."

He also produced *An Anti-Suffrage Alphabet*,[6] a parody of children's ABC books, in which each letter documented the subjugation of women without the vote, such as W is for Washing "which woman must do day in & day out & on polling day too". It was created with Leonora Tyson from the WSPU; the illustrations were coloured in the WSPU's trademark colours of purple, white and green, and the book was sold to raise funds for their campaigns. Housman also designed banners for WSPU members to carry on their marches.

Another early member of the Men's League was Israel Zangwill, who had achieved success in Britain and overseas for his novel *Children of the Ghetto*, published in 1892, and had become a recognized authority on the social problems of the East End of London as well as on discrimination and other issues that affected Jewish people in Britain. He joined soon after the League was founded and is remembered for his inspirational writing and speeches about universal suffrage.

Emmeline Pethick-Lawrence explained why the WSPU had adopted their colours: "Purple, as everyone knows, is the royal colour. It stands for the royal blood that flows in the veins of every suffragette, the instinct of freedom and dignity ... white stands for purity in private and public life ... green is the colour of hope and the emblem of spring." The phrase "Votes for Women" had become the battle-cry of the WSPU, adopted as the title of their magazine. The first issue of the WSPU magazine was published in 1907 and the posters advertising it were emblazoned with white, purple and green illustrations. *Votes for Women* would grow to have tens of thousands of subscribers and its

---

6. A copy of the book can be seen in the collection at the Museum of London.

articles would disseminate the suffragette message all over the country. The magazine featured articles and illustrations by members of the WSPU and prominent "names" in the suffrage community. It was sold by women vendors standing on the street in their prominent "Votes for Women" sashes and, by the 1910s, in WSPU shops.

The NUWSS adopted their own colours of white, green and red. As the two groups wore, intentionally, such similar colours, the image of the suffragette and the suffragist became a well-known one. All over the country, women and girls could be seen wearing clothing and accessories echoing one or other of the colour schemes: white dresses with green and purple or green and red sashes were a common sight, as were hats, gloves, fans and other accessories in suffragette or suffragist colours. Fashion houses and jewellers were happy to exploit the market, producing a variety of items aimed at WSPU or NUWSS members. Suffragettes and suffragists continued to make plans for campaigns that would catch the public eye. Following the failure of the Women's Parliament, Lady Harberton, a pioneer of the Radical Dress movement, suggested that suffragists should dress up in men's clothing to gain access to the House of Commons. As one journalist commented:

"The idea, however, was not only thought of long ago, but was put into practice. There were 'ructions' in 1779, after which women were excluded from the House of Commons for many years; but the beautiful Mrs Sheridan went disguised as a man to hear her husband speak, and the Duchess of Gordon adopted the same trick with equal success. But the modern policeman is a 'knowing bird', and it would seem that the Suffragists would run the double risk of being charged with wrongfully wearing male attire, as well as rioting, if they adopt such a stratagem in their next organised descent upon the House of Commons."

As the suffrage movement gained in forced, so did the anti-suffrage movement, and during the first decade of the 20th century there were regular debates and rallies held by both sides. In March 1907, a Women's Suffrage Bill had been introduced in Parliament – but it was beset by so much deliberate prevarication in the House of Commons that its proposers ran out of time and the bill failed. That year there was a small, if slightly hollow-sounding, victory, however, when a change in legislation granted women permission to run as a candidate in local elections and to be elected mayor.[7] The first female mayor to be elected in England was Dr Elizabeth Garrett Anderson. The anti-suffrage league felt that this was what women should be content with and were vociferous in airing their belief that women should now be content with their lot and stop agitating for more change. As a result, a number of debates were set up between local suffrage and anti-suffrage societies.

In 1907, a debate in Reigate, in Surrey, prompted Miss Rendel, a speaker from the Central Suffrage Society, to face up to the issue that many women did not know anything about politics – this was a subject that needed to be addressed as it was used so often as an argument against women being given the vote. In her speech she asked, "Why is it so? Because they have been shut out of political life and thought, and not allowed to understand." She exhorted women to make it their duty to become more politically aware, telling them to ask their "husbands and fathers and brothers to explain politics to them, and so fit themselves for their duties in the future".

Two years later a heated debate took place in Bath, in Somerset, with Miss Edith Wheelwright, the Hon. Secretary of the Bath Women's Suffrage Society, going head to head with Miss Price of the Clifton Anti-Suffrage League. The local newspaper reported the debate with glee:

"Miss Wheelwright's argument was that the necessity for the woman's vote had increased under the conditions of an industrial democracy, wherein legislation interfered so largely with women's work, which was in the main, unprotected, unrepresented, and under-paid. She referred to the progress of the Suffrage movement in the European countries; notable in Germany, Italy, and the Scandinavian lands; also to the high testimony from the Colonies as to the excellent effect of the women's vote upon home legislation."

---

7. On 21 May 1908, a dinner was held at the Empire Rooms in the Trocadero in London for the newly elected women town councillors, and to raise funds for the suffrage cause.

In response to Miss Wheelwright's speech, Miss Price was reported to have said that she "thought that the affairs of an important Empire like England should be left to men, as the ultimate authority rested with the men, whose physical force (even shown in the building of bridges and making of roads) was the foundation of civilised government.... She considered that women might be unsexed by contact with the questionable methods of politics."

The idea that women could be "unsexed" by emancipation was an argument that had been raging for many years. Queen Victoria had expressed the same fear in a letter to her friend Theodore Martin[8] several decades earlier. In 1908, Martin published a book entitled *Queen Victoria as I Knew Her*, weighing into the suffrage debate with the revelation that the monarch had written to him in 1870 (talking about herself in the third person as was usual) to say: "It is a subject which makes the Queen so furious that she cannot contain herself. God created men and women different – then let them remain each in their own position.... Woman would become the most hateful, heartless and disgusting of human beings were she allowed to unsex herself; and where would be the protection which man was intended to give the weaker sex?" To ensure there would be no suffrage nonsense in the Martins' own home, the letter-writer ended her comments with: "The Queen is sure that Mrs Martin agrees with her."

In Bath in 1909, in response to Miss Price's comments about men's important "physical force" and women being "unsexed" by suffrage, a local suffragist named Miss Severs replied that: "the physical force of women is scarcely a negligible quality, inasmuch as the race could not go on without it." The suffragists won the debate by 19 votes to 5 in support of Miss Price (although several audience members chose not to vote at all).

---

8. Theodore Martin was a Scottish writer commissioned by Queen Victoria to write a posthumous biography of Prince Albert. She was so pleased with the resulting book that she knighted him. They remained friends to the end of her life.

The WSPU set up its own shops, with the flagship store at 39 West Street in Reading, Berkshire (it would open in 1910). Women were asked to support the shops both as customers and as volunteer workers. The shops were also used as meeting places and as advice centres for women in need. The Reading shop was run by Mrs Margesson, who arranged meetings at times when working women would be able to attend. The WSPU commissioned a large number of items to be sold at their shops and meetings, from suffragette fashions to WSPU-branded tea, jam, chocolate, stationery and literature. One of their most popular items was a board game named "Pank-a-Squith", [9] the object of which was to move the figure of a suffragette from her home to the Houses of Parliament, whilst attempting to avoid obstacles along the way. The design of the game took the form of a spiral, with "home" at the outside and the Houses of Parliament in the middle. There were six suffragette figures (allowing up to six players) and the problems they encountered along the way included police brutality, prison and force-feeding. It was played on the principal of Snakes and Ladders, with certain squares causing the suffragette to miss a turn or, for example, have to go back home and start again in order to avoid the police. One square depicted suffragettes hurling stones through the windows of the Home Office; another showed them chaining themselves to railings. The first player to make it to the square in the centre achieved universal suffrage. Other WSPU merchandise included the board game "In and Out of Prison" and a card game named "Panko or Votes for Women", described as "the great card game: Suffragists v Anti-Suffragists".

---

9. A Pank-a-Squith game can be seen in the collections at the Museum of London and the People's History Museum in Manchester.

Chapter Fifteen

"The time is fast coming – coming at motor speed – when in no civilised country will be seen cars without electricity or women without the vote."

Israel Zangwill, from his speech made on 7 June 1909

Throughout the early months of 1908 there was great excitement amongst all suffragists and suffragettes, as the Liberal MP Henry Stanger introduced a private member's bill on women's suffrage. The bill passed two readings – before being blocked by the government. That political blow, and its resultant humiliation as anti-suffrage campaigners gloated about the defeat, made the WSPU, NUWSS and all their affiliated societies even more determined to make the country pay attention.

In June, two mass women's suffrage demonstrations took place in London. The first, on 14 June, was a suffragist rally organized by the NUWSS, which attracted more than 10,000 supporters from all over the country. The organizers ensured that all those who wanted to come were able to do so, and that everyone was provided with food and drink. As was usual for the suffrage societies, the NUWSS paid the train fares of those who wanted to attend but could not afford the journey to London. The suffragists marched through the streets of central London, carrying banners and singing, before ending up at the Royal Albert Hall in South Kensington, where speeches were delivered and new friendships were forged. Those who took part described the exhilaration of being amongst so many like-minded women all in one place. It was an unforgettable day.

The suffragettes' event took place a week later, on 21 June, and, to the fury of the anti-suffrage movement, attracted even more attendees than the NUWSS event. The WSPU demonstration and rally was organized by Christabel Pankhurst. During the build-up to what it dubbed "Suffrage Sunday", *Votes for Women* kept the women informed and rallied them to the cause: "The Twenty-first of June will be the longest day in 1908, and it will be the day in 1908 longest remembered." The paper exhorted its supporters not only to come themselves but to bring with them as many other people – men and women – as they could in order to swell the numbers, and to encourage "hesistants" to join the cause. Under the headline "The Waitresses", an article in the 4 June paper also demonstrated how far the women's movement had moved from its working-class origins:

> *"We find that the teashop girls and waitresses are intensely interested in the question of women's suffrage, but it is a very difficult matter to come into touch with them. A great deal of good might be done in that direction if each of our members made a point of visiting every teashop in their district, and distributing bills referring to the Hyde Park demonstration.... This is the only way by which we can hope to bring a large number of waitresses with us to Hyde Park. We hope that none of our members will lose an opportunity of working in this manner. Many women are taking one and some two meals a day in teashops."*

The newspaper also held reports of WSPU speakers being allowed to hold meetings at workplaces such as a furniture shop and nurses' quarters, spreading the message to as many women as possible and asking them to join in the march on Women's Sunday. The union had printed out a quarter of a million cards or "tickets" with all the details of the march for members to hand out. They had been produced to emulate railway tickets and were handed out at stations to men taking commuter trains, in the hope that they and their wives and sisters would be converted to the cause and march through the streets with the WSPU members.

It was estimated that 25,000 women marched through London that Sunday, on their way to the rally in Hyde Park. So many different groups were represented that they carried between them more than 700 banners.[1] Many women were dressed in WSPU colours and Dr Diane Atkinson writes in her book *Votes for Women*: "The wealthier women took the wearing of the colours so seriously that department stores in London sold out of white dresses and purple, white and green accessories well before the day."

The marchers sang specially written songs, such as that by L. Nightingale which included the words:

> *"March, women, march! While free and brave*
> *Your brilliant banners float and wave;*
> *The blue sky bends benignantly –*
> *March, women, march to Victory."*

It was not only the WSPU who marched that day: other suffrage societies also took part, proudly carrying the banners of their individual societies. One of the most "brilliant banners" was held by the men and women of the Fabian Society, having been created specially by the

---

1. Figure from the Greater London Authority archive.

talented needlewoman and designer May Morris, one of the daughters of William Morris and his wife Janey.

Flushed by the success of "Suffrage Sunday", the WSPU organized another demonstration on the final day of June. It took place in Parliament Square and was attended not only by thousands of supporters but also by thousands of police officers. The demonstration soon turned into a violent clash between police and suffragettes – with several gangs of men weighing in on the side of the police and assaulting the women. The police allowed them to do so. It was believed that the new Prime Minister Herbert Henry Asquith had granted permission to the police to use deliberate violence and intimidation against the women. As a furious response to the police brutality, two suffragettes (both school teachers) took a cab to 10 Downing Street, the official residence of the Prime Minister, where they threw stones through two of his windows. The age of the "window smasher" had begun.

The names of the first window smashers were Mary Leigh and Edith New. They were sent to prison, along with 25 other suffragettes arrested that day in Parliament Square. For their violation of the Prime Minister's house, the two school teachers were sentenced to two months (in Holloway Prison, a gaol that would become synonymous with the suffragette movement). The two women were fêted as heroines to the cause. The treatment they received in prison was despised and described as having been of "the greatest possible severity". An article in the *Manchester Courier* described the day of their release:

> "Drizzling rain rendered the gate of Holloway by no means a pleasant rendezvous at eight o'clock. Nevertheless the Suffragettes gathered in force, in white summer dresses with the familiar purple, white, and green sashes bearing the words 'Vote for Women'. A few minutes after eight the prisoners were released, their appearance being the signal for loud cheers from the crowd that had

assembled several hundred strong. Bouquets and kisses were showered on the two ladies, who were immediately escorted to a brougham which was in waiting, a band meanwhile striking up the 'Marseillaise'. A procession was formed and a demonstrative march commenced to Queen's Hall, where breakfast had been prepared. The prisoners were drawn by a team of Suffragettes attached to the brougham."

The breakfast was presided over by Christabel Pankhurst who gave a rousing speech praising the released prisoners' actions. She commented that it had taken the women's movement 40 years before anyone had thought of throwing stones as a protest, and that Mary Leigh and Edith New had been responsible for helping to move the campaign forward dramatically. She described the stone-throwing as "the whitest and purest moments of their lives". The two guests of honour also made speeches and Edith New related how she had induced the prison librarian to allow her to read Shakespeare and had selected a new motto for the women's movement: "Out of the nettle of danger we pluck the flower of safety". This was greeted with rousing cheers.

Once the excitement of their release had died down, however, the revulsion over the way the two women had been treated was discussed at length. The government, it was believed, was insisting that suffragette prisoners should be humiliated, belittled and treated violently. Many prisoners related shocking stories of physical violence and bullying from the prison staff.

Clashes between police and the suffragettes were to become a constant fixture in the newspapers. In 1909, Millicent Garrett Fawcett wrote to Lady Frances Balfour about violent scenes she had witnessed between women and the police. She was frightened, but in awe of the militant suffragettes: "The physical courage of it all is intensely moving," she wrote. In addition to window-smashing, suffragettes began to protest by chaining themselves to railings, attempting to hit government ministers with horse-whips, disrupting sporting events and making constant attempts to get inside the Houses of Parliament, including one famous time when they hid inside a van purportedly making a delivery; the press dubbed it "the Trojan Horse incident". Other tactics included groups of arrested suffragettes all giving the same name to confuse the police, disrupting church services and local government meetings with impromptu speeches about women's rights, vandalizing golf courses and racecourses, setting fire to post-boxes and generally trying to cause disruption to everyday life. As the movement gained both momentum and fury, this militant action would extend to include attacks on private homes and property. Assaults on government offices became commonplace, and demonstrations and violent acts began to take place all over the country. The cells at Holloway and other prisons were permanently occupied with female prisoners, and suffrage magazines and newspapers were filled with descriptions of prison brutality. Journalists reporting on trials of suffragettes commented that many of them appeared in court with a ready-packed suitcase, fully intending to ignore the fines and go straight to prison. It was only a matter of time before the women began a new type of protest.

When the authorities continued to refuse to recognize the women's call to be treated as political prisoners, one woman decided to act. The artist Marion Wallace Dunlop had been arrested for "wilful damage". Her crime was that she had attached a "Bill of Rights" to the wall of St Stephen's Hall at the Palace of Westminster. *The Times* reported that the poster objected to the treatment of suffrage campaigners, pointing out that such treatment was unconstitutional. Under the title "Women's Deputation", the bill proclaimed: "It is the right of the subjects to petition the King, and all commitments and prosecutions for such petitionings are illegal."

At Wallace Dunlop's trial she was ordered to pay a fine of £5 plus the cost of the damage she had caused, which was reported to have been assessed as £1 1s 2d.[2] She refused to pay and, in the summer of 1909, was sent to Holloway Prison. There she made the decision to refuse to eat, beginning the very first suffragette "hunger strike". Christabel Pankhurst later released a statement claiming that, on entering the prison, Marion Wallace Dunlop had written to the Prime Minister requesting that she be granted political prisoner status and announcing that she would not eat until she had been granted that right. Her hunger strike lasted for a reported 91 hours before the prison authorities, uncertain of how to deal with her protest and unwilling to cope with the bad publicity of a suffragette starving within their walls, conceded defeat and released her. Although the WSPU had not known beforehand that Wallace Dunlop would start this form of protest, the union rapidly adopted it as its own and from this time onwards, the newspapers carried regular stories about hunger-striking suffrage prisoners.

When force-feeding of suffragettes became commonplace, an aristocratic member of WSPU, Lady Constance Lytton,[3] became suspicious that she was being treated differently from her working-class peers purely because of her elevated social status. She heard reports of terrible brutality, yet when she was imprisoned and went on hunger strike, she was released after only a couple of days, having endured no force-feeding. Lady Constance decided to go undercover to investigate, so she assumed a new identity, that of a poor, working-class woman named Jane Warton. She was arrested – as Jane Warton – while on a demonstration. This time she discovered the truth, as she was force-fed with great brutality and treated with contempt. In her 1996 article on force-feeding for the *Times Higher Education*, the historian Jane Purvis commented:

> *"This time Jane Warton enjoyed none of the courtesies shown to Lady Lytton. Warton was held down by wardresses as the doctor inserted a four-foot-long tube down her throat. A few seconds after the tube was down,*

---

2. Other sources set the damages at 10 shillings, but the court reports written up by the press state £1 1s 2d.

3. Lady Constance Lytton was the granddaughter of the Victorian writer Edward Bulwer Lytton and his estranged wife Rosina (see p.43).

she vomited all over her hair, her clothes and the wall, yet the task continued until all the liquid had been emptied into her stomach."[4]

In 1914, the book *Prisons and Prisoners: Some Personal Experiences* was published under the authorship of "Constance Lytton and Jane Warton, Spinster". In her memoirs, Constance Lytton recalled:

> *"I was sick over the doctor and the wardresses, and it seemed a long time before they took the tube out. As the doctor left he gave me a slap on the cheek, not violent, but, as it were, to express his contemptuous disapproval, and he seemed to take for granted that my distress was assumed. At first it seemed such an utterly contemptible thing to have done that I could only laugh in my mind. Then suddenly I saw Jane Warton lying before me, and it seemed as if I were outside of her. She was the most despised, ignorant and helpless prisoner that I had seen. When she had served her time and was out of the prison, no one would believe anything she said…. That was Jane Warton, and I had come to help her."*

---

4. In 2008, playwright Rebecca Lenkiewicz's play *Her Naked Skin* premiered in London. The play is set in Holloway Prison in 1913 and features harrowing scenes of rape-like force-feeding of suffragettes. It was intended to shock and to be controversial, but there was also a modern shocking fact associated with the play. The National Theatre in London was opened in 1976 and houses several theatre spaces. It boasts over 1,000 performances per year, yet despite over 30 years of history, *Her Naked Skin* marked the first time that a full-length play written by a woman made it to the Oliver Theatre – the largest stage within the National Theatre.

When the prison authorities discovered the true identity of "Jane Warton", she was released with haste – but the physical damage caused by these assaults in prison was irreversible. Constance Lytton's health had never been robust and it was permanently destroyed by the brutal treatment she had received in prison. Her memoirs include the comment: "I lay quite motionless, it seemed paradise to be without the suffocating tube, without the liquid food going in and out of my body and without the gag between my teeth." The next time she was force-fed she was sick again over the doctor, the same man who had slapped her. He yelled furiously that if she vomited on him again he would "feed you twice". Two years after her imprisonment, Constance Lytton suffered a stroke. She never recovered fully and died on 22 May 1923 at the age of 54. Other suffragettes also left harrowing accounts of the health problems they suffered as a result of the force-feeding, not least the infections caused by filthy, shared feeding tubes. In several prisons, many women were force-fed rectally, turning the already terrifying practice into rape.

It was not only female suffragists who were force-fed. Several men who were imprisoned for the suffrage cause also went on hunger strike and received the same treatment as the female prisoners. Christabel Pankhurst took up the case of Mr Ball, a man who had been imprisoned in 1911 for throwing a stone through a window at the Home Office. After visiting him, his wife had been so concerned about his health that she requested an independent, non-prison doctor visit him in prison, but her request was refused. Christabel went to the papers to tell them that not only was he was on hunger strike and had been forcibly fed but the prison authorities had written to Mrs Ball telling her that they intended to certify her husband as "insane". The WSPU insisted that two "eminent specialists", of their own choosing, not the prison's, should be allowed to examine him. Christabel also pointed out that if he were insane, that should have been noticed by the prison at the start, not the end, of his sentence and his medical treatment should have been very different from that which he had received. At a suffragette demonstration, with journalists present, Christabel announced, "Before his imprisonment Mr Ball was a healthy, athletic man. If he is not now sane he must have been driven insane by his treatment within prison." The WSPU hoped that if men realized other men were being tortured in prison, they might be prompted to join the campaign to help end such brutality.

In 1912, the Russian actress Princess Bariatinsky gave a speech at an Adult Suffrage meeting in Glasgow (presided over by Christabel Pankhurst and the Labour leader Keir Hardie). The *Dundee Courier* reported the speech made by the actress:

"Speaking in excellent English, she said she came from a country where tyranny in its vilest shape reigned supreme…. To her, a Russian woman, it was incomprehensible that British people, who had always been in the forefront in the struggle for freedom, should refuse to make women citizens in the fullest sense." Princess Bariatinsky also talked about the brutality political prisoners suffered in Russia and called upon the British government to stop supporting such a "tyrannical" regime. Many women who attended the meeting believed that the suffragettes in prison were enduring similar treatment to the political prisoners in Russia.

Campaigning suffragettes were awarded medals of honour by the WSPU and other groups. Those who had been to prison were presented with a silver badge depicting a prison gate and chains; those who had endured hunger strike were given the same badge in a larger size; and those who suffered force-feeding were given the same large badge but with a silver bar across the ribbon.

One of the most famous suffragettes to endure force-feeding was Flora Drummond, one of Emmeline Pankhurst's closest supporters and known in the WSPU as "the General". In 1908, she was sent a gift by what the WSPU described as "an enterprising firm who had heard of her new official title". The gift was a military-style "fine regalia of white velvet bordered with gold braid. It is hand-embroidered in purple and green, with the word 'General' and our familiar battle-cry." (*Votes for Women*, 4 June 1908). In her obituary, it was claimed that although Drummond bore the force-feeding stoically, returning repeatedly to prison to re-endure the suffering, she "bore the scars to the grave". In an interview given shortly before she died (in 1949), she commented:

"There are a lot of us with marks still upon us, through kicks and other ill-treatment all those years ago."

Flora Drummond's innovative and often witty campaigns became legendary amongst the suffragettes. They included hiring a boat so she could position herself on the River Thames directly in line with the terrace of the Houses of Parliament and harangue MPs via a megaphone. She also had the idea of sending suffragettes "by parcel post" to 10 Downing Street. In 1930, Flora Drummond would be present at Victoria Tower Gardens in London to witness the unveiling of a statue to Emmeline Pankhurst – she commented that they were standing just a short distance from the railings to which she and Mrs Pankhurst had once chained themselves in protest. Also present at the ceremony was Stanley Baldwin, the Prime Minister who had finally granted women the vote. Flora Drummond looked around at the crowds and said to Baldwin, "Half the women here are gaol-birds!"

Chapter Sixteen

"The Suffragettes may have been treated badly by the Liberals. That is not the point. They have no excuse whatever for wanton wickedness. All law-abiding and self-respecting people abhor such tactics. They detract from the dignity with which we associate womanhood. They unpopularise a cause which is absolutely sound in principle."

"Women on the Warpath", *Dundee Courier*, 23 November 1910

By the end of 1909, Asquith had enjoyed almost two years as Prime Minister and was leading the Liberals into a campaign before the next general election, in January 1910. During his pre-election campaigning, he pledged that, if the Liberals were returned to office, a vote would be held about adding an amendment on women's suffrage to the Reform Bill, implying that property-holding women would finally be given the vote. Once elected, he reneged on this promise. Even during the election campaign, women were growing weary of what they believed was mere rhetoric with no conviction behind it. In March 1909, the front cover of *Votes for Women* had featured a cartoon of disillusioned suffragettes leaving a theatre while a puppet of Asquith performed a dance on stage. The puppet was holding up a placard stating "Votes for Everyone" and saying, "This ought to be a good show." The suffragettes responded with the words, "It is a trick we can see through." As usual, the signature of the cartoonist was given as "A. Patriot" (*Votes for Women*, 12 March 1909).

After it became apparent that Asquith had betrayed them, both suffragists and suffragettes stepped up their campaigns. Emmeline Pankhurst rallied women with the words: "Our power as women is invincible if we are united and determined." On 18 November 1910, the violence against suffragettes reached a new and terrifying low. The date is now remembered in history as "Black Friday", a day on which the police and any anti-suffrage men who cared to join in were permitted – and encouraged – to use not only violence but also sexual violence against the women.

Earlier that year, the WSPU had agreed to suspend all militant action because resolution had seemed finally at hand. In June 1910, an all-party committee of pro-suffrage MPs had drafted the Conciliation Bill, which had been introduced and passed by a majority of 110 – yet in the autumn, Asquith refused to allow the facilities for making the Bill law, on the grounds that the Bill as it stood was "not capable of free amendment". The statement released to the newspapers stated baldly: "The Prime Minister ... says the time at the disposal of the Government will not admit of further progress being made with the Woman Suffrage Bill this year. As regards facilities next year, Mr Asquith hopes to be able to make a statement before very long." Once again, the Prime Minister had shown disregard for non-militant, political attempts to change the law. The WSPU and NUWSS were united in their disgust for his treatment of the issue.

During the time when the Bill was going through Parliament, the police had been issued with special guidelines:

> *"In view of the probability of further 'Militant' action on the part of members of the various Suffrage Societies in connection with the Bill now before Parliament, the following instructions are circulated.*

Any of these persons standing outside the residence of a Minister or taking up a fixed position in close proximity thereto on the footway so as to cause annoyance to such Minister, irrespective of obstruction being caused or placards exhibited, are to be cautioned that their presence is calculated to cause annoyance or obstruction, and they are to be requested to depart.

If they do not leave, they are to be further informed that Police in the exercise of their duties cannot allow them to remain, and that if they continue to remain, it will be necessary to take them into custody and charge them with wilfully obstructing or resisting Police in the execution of their duty....

Experienced Officers who may be relied upon to exercise discretion and forbearance are to be employed, and their duties are to be carefully and fully explained to them.

It is not desirable that arrests should be made if that course can be obviated, but Police are, nevertheless, to be instructed to act with firmness as well as with tact."[1]

On 18 November, after hearing the news that the first Conciliation Bill had failed, Elizabeth Garrett Anderson[2] and Emmeline Pankhurst

---

1. Police memorandum on Suffragettes, 11 July 1910, now held in the National Archives at Kew.

2. Despite the fact that her sister was President of the NUWSS, Elizabeth Garrett Anderson had allied herself to the WSPU and become friends with the charismatic Emmeline Pankhurst.

led a deputation of women on a march to the House of Commons. The march was in protest at Asquith's refusal to recognize the Bill, despite the fact that it had been approved by the majority of MPs. Their intention was for the leaders to request a meeting with the Prime Minister, and present him with a "memorial protesting against the policy of delay" and requesting him to "immediately withdraw the veto which has been placed upon the Women's Suffrage Bill". The day's events started in Caxton Hall in Westminster, which had been used for WSPU events since 1907.[3] There had been a great deal of publicity in the days leading up to the event and the government had obviously prepared as minutely as the suffrage campaigners had done. A mark of how the day would turn out can be seen in the statement issued by the Press Association, printed in newspapers on the morning of 18 November: "If Women Suffragists raid the House of Commons to-day, it is confidently predicted that the police may be compelled to make a larger number of arrests than on previous occasions."

It was estimated that around 300 WSPU and NUWSS members crowded into Caxton Hall, together with a smaller number of male supporters. They all wore suffrage colours as well as a small silk badge bearing the words "Deputation, 1910". Emmeline Pethick-Lawrence presided over the meeting at which several prominent members made "inspiring" speeches, as one pro-suffrage journalist reported, and Flora Drummond was appointed "Commander-in-Chief". Although most newspaper reports write about an unruly mob of hundreds of women descending *en masse* upon Parliament, the reality was very different. At Caxton Hall the marchers were divided into groups of no more than 13 people, with Flora Drummond supervising who went in each group and in what order they would start to march. Each group would leave separately, with departures at staggered intervals.

The first group to leave carried the suffrage banners and the words

---

3. During October and November 1910, Caxton Hall was also used by the controversial writer and occultist Aleister Crowley, to perform his work *The Rites of Eleusis*.

of the memorial to be delivered to Asquith. Their job was to get to the gates of the House of Commons and in so doing be well placed to get inside and speak to the Prime Minister, with whom they had requested an audience. In this group were several of the most prominent and well-respected suffrage campaigners – although most of their names are little remembered today. Emmeline Pankhurst walked with Dr Elizabeth Garrett Anderson and her daughter Dr Louisa Garrett Anderson, together with Mrs Mansell Mullin, Mrs Saul Solomon, Mrs May, Mrs Lowy, Mrs Willcock, Mrs Darrant Harrison, Mrs Chilnail, the engineer Mrs Hertha Ayrton[4], Sophia Duleep Singh and Mrs Brackenbury (who was in her seventies and mentioned in the newspapers as "the wife of General Brackenbury"). Sophia Duleep Singh was the British-born daughter of the former Maharajah of the Punjab; she was a member of the Tax Resistance League and one of the most active members of the Richmond (Surrey) WSPU. Ironically, she lived in a "grace and favour" apartment at Hampton Court, bestowed upon her by Queen Victoria a few years before the anti-suffragist monarch's death.

Amongst the many people who gathered in Caxton Hall were a group of Irish women, who received "a special cheer of encouragement" from the crowd as they set on their way; suffragists who had travelled from America and Australia; Mary Taylor, the granddaughter of John Stuart Mill; and Mrs Cobden-Sanderson, a daughter of the reforming MP Richard Cobden. The London correspondent for the *Derby Chronicle* wrote: "Most of the ladies were well dressed. I saw some being led away who were dressed in furs, and the sight of a constable on either side of one of these was incongruous." (He wrote of the crowd outside the hall: "Some of the unemployed swelled the multitude, and some light-fingered gentry were there, too.")

The London correspondent for the *Western Times* wrote that the

---

4. Hertha Ayrton (born Phoebe Marks) was the first women to address the Royal Society and the first female member of the Institution of Electrical Engineers. Her husband, William Ayrton, was a renowned physicist.

marchers walked unimpeded as far Westminster Abbey:

> *"Here, however, a band of roughs offered obstacles to further progress, roughly jostling the women, while they jeered and yelled with delight at their discomfiture. Undaunted, the ladies persevered, and, though roughly handled in the mêlée, presently joined forces with the banner-bearers lined up outside St Stephen's entrance. This was the signal for renewed hustling of a shameful character. The banners were torn down and trampled in the grass to the accompaniment of rude taunts, but headway was still made, till the Suffragettes at last, gaining St Stephen's entrance, found the way being barred by adamantine police. The women waited patiently in the hope that an interview would be granted."*

Another journalist wrote sneeringly: "large bodies of police had been drafted into Westminster to give the ladies and their friends a fitting reception."

Asquith had no intention of meeting the protestors. Instead it seems that he had instructed the police not to arrest the women at first, but to treat them with violence instead. As the women tried to push forwards, they were kicked, punched, pinched and had knees – or in some cases groping hands – thrust between their thighs. Police grabbed women's hands and bent back their thumbs or fingers, twisted their wrists and deliberately shoved the women into the way of oncoming vehicles and crowds. One of the most widespread methods of assault was for police to grab women by the chest and twist their breasts agonizingly. It was not only the police who molested the women: a mob of male anti-suffrage protesters joined in and the police did nothing to stop them assaulting the women. One woman later reported back to the WSPU that when she had told a policeman he was assaulting her, he replied maliciously that he was allowed to "grip you wherever I like today", which led to the suspicion that the police had been told to use sexual violence as a form of crowd control.

Many of the women believed that some of the "mob" were actually policemen out of uniform. On 25 November, *Votes for Women* reported: "The orders of the Home Secretary were, apparently, that the police were to be present both in uniform and also in plain clothes among the crowd and that the women were to be thrown from one to the other." Hertha Ayrton left this description of the day:

> *"Before any of us could get into the House, we had to run the gauntlet of organised gangs of policemen in plain clothes, dressed like roughs, who nearly squeezed the breath out of our bodies, the policemen in official clothes helping them. I nearly fainted and Louisa Garrett-Anderson succeeded in making them let me through. Mrs Saul Solomon was seized by the breasts and thrown down."*

Hugh Franklin, a member of the Men's League for Women's Suffrage, recorded: "The police, acting under orders, instead of arresting the women and protecting like they have done on previous occasions, threw them to the mob."[5]

After the events of Black Friday, the activists Henry Brailsford and Dr Jessie Murray interviewed those who had been in Parliament Square. The resulting report makes for harrowing reading.[6] One woman, identified only as Miss C, reported that a policeman had lifted up her skirt before throwing her into the crowd "and incited the men to treat me as they wished". The police were no respecters of age: one elderly

---

5. Hugh Franklin quotation from the Women's Library article "Black Friday Centenary", 2010.

6. The Brailsford and Murray report is now at the British Library in London.

lady thought that the policeman who gripped her so hard she could not breathe was going to kill her. She saw the look on his face change from maliciousness to fear as he realized "he had gone too far". Less than two months after Black Friday, she suffered a heart attack and died. The WSPU laid the blame for her death directly at the hands of the police. Perhaps the most vicious of all the stories that Murray and Brailsford collected was that of May Billinghurst, who was disabled and unable to move without her invalid carriage. After disabling the wheels on her carriage so that she was unable to escape, police carried her to a side street, beat her up and left her in the middle of "a hooligan crowd".

Towards the end of day, Elizabeth Garrett Anderson sent a postcard to her sister Millicent Garrett Fawcett[7] stating that about 70 people had been arrested, that she had been "steered through the crowd" by her son Alan but that her daughter Louisa was "staying on to the end". Witnesses claimed that 150 suffragettes were hurt in the violence.[8] When those who had escaped arrest found their way back to Caxton Hall, the stories of violence were almost overwhelming. Many related how they had been dragged into side streets and beaten up. The doctors and nurses, who had been waiting for them to return and expecting some injuries, were shocked by the extent of the brutality.

In 1913, Rebecca West wrote about Black Friday in an article for *The Clarion* in which she not only points the blame at the police but also at women from the anti-suffrage movement: "[I] saw the police assaulting a woman who would not give them a tricolour flag she was holding. They bent her backwards and shook her by the shoulders,

---

7. Biographers Jo Manton and Ray Strachey record the story that Millicent Garrett Fawcett was so distressed at the thought of her 70-year-old sister attending the march, telling Lady Frances Balfour that Elizabeth was too old and frail to cope with being handled violently or arrested, that Lady Balfour used her influence with the Home Secretary and gained the assurance that no one would arrest or molest Mrs Garrett Anderson. This both relieved and appalled Millicent, as an example that power could be "bought" by personal influence.

8. Figure from the People's History Museum in Manchester.

sawing away with their nails at her hands so that she might drop the flagstaff. On each side of me stood a group of women applauding this demonstration of the chivalry of man and the weakness of women."

Elizabeth Garrett Anderson's estimate of 70 arrests was well under the official figure: when the defendants appeared in court the following day, the papers reported that 115 women and 4 men had been arrested on Black Friday (the name given to the day by the suffragettes, not by the newspapers, who did not use the term). The news rapidly spread overseas and the WSPU received letters and telegrams of encouragement from supporters of women's suffrage around the world. Ironically, Black Friday took place at about the same time as the US state of Washington granted its women the vote. As soon as word reached them about the events in London, an American suffrage society sent a telegram to say: "We honor you and suffer with you. Organising sympathy fund here."

Those arrested were taken to Bow Street Magistrates' Court on Saturday, 19 November, where it was announced that Winston Churchill, the Home Secretary, had agreed none would be charged (except for those who had broken windows) and none would be imprisoned. Churchill's statement said that he felt there would be "no public advantage" to prosecuting so many. It was, however, not Churchill's finest hour and he was lampooned from all sides. As he was considered by the suffragists to be responsible – jointly with Asquith – for the police practising sexual assault as a form of law-keeping, the women did not feel kindly disposed towards him. Nor did the general public, who were sure that he was being far too lenient and there would be repercussions as a result. Many newspapers printed furious articles denouncing Churchill's decision.[9] *Votes for Women* reported that the WSPU was now in "a state of war".

-----

9. In an un-prophetic article in which Rebecca West was scathing about politicians' treatment of the suffragettes, she wrote of "Mr Churchill, that pathetic figure whose lack of political success is an eternal warning to opportunists that there are some souls for which the devil does not care to pay a price".

It seems likely Churchill made his decision with the aim of avoiding investigations into police actions during the protest – his refusal to prosecute meant that none of the defendants were able, or expected, to speak from the witness box – as well as refusing to give the WSPU the publicity they craved by sending any of their members (or their leader) to prison. Emmeline Pankhurst nimbly turned the Home Secretary's decision to her advantage. If he had hoped to wrong-foot her, Churchill was unsuccessful. When interviewed by the clamouring group of reporters, she announced that, "the release of the defendants was a great triumph for the suffrage cause, and convinced them that victory was at hand. It was an admission of the great injustice practised by the Government in the past in imprisoning many women for long periods as common criminals for the same action as that taken by the deputation yesterday."

Many of the women had arrived at the court with bags ready packed for prison, and newspapers commented that some of them looked disappointed to have been deprived of their protest, while others looked relieved and some thanked the magistrate. One young woman was noticed to have been "clutching a large box of chocolates" which the journalist surmised she was intending to console herself with on the journey to Holloway Prison and possible hunger striking.

The events of Black Friday had the effect of swinging public opinion more firmly in support of the suffrage movement. Sylvia Pankhurst had been at the demonstration in the role of reporter for *Votes for Women*. In her article she wrote: "Never ... have I seen so much bravery on the part of the women and so much violent brutality on the part of the policemen ... and some men in plain clothes." Most of the large newspapers were keen to report on the wounds suffered by policemen, but even in the most outraged reports these seemed to amount merely to twisted ankles, damaged uniforms and bruises from being kicked. While the big papers toed the government line, many of the local papers, as well as the journalists who had been present in Parliament Square, were appalled by what they had witnessed. Soon there was a loud voice calling for a public inquiry into police brutality towards the women. Winston Churchill refused. When Henry Brailsford and

Dr Jessie Murray produced their report into the day's events, they passed it on, via the Conciliation Committee, to the Home Office, but Churchill still refused an investigation. He knew that a public enquiry could not exonerate the police and would give the suffragettes far too much public sympathy.

That public support for the suffragettes had grown was evident at an event held at the WSPU shop in Bath several weeks after Black Friday. A local suffragette, Miss S. Strangeways, talked about her recollections of the day and described the treatment the women received as being "a stain on the honour of England". In response, a local clergyman, the Rev. C. Stuart Smith, surprised the attending journalist by defending the actions of the militant suffrage movement. He said that he prayed for the militants and commented:

> "The time for using constitutional methods in the women's movement has passed.... Women, not being citizens, have no right to constitutional methods ... so they must use the same methods men used before they were made citizens.... The women who break glass are those who have come to feel their present position absolutely intolerable. The only place for an honest woman now is prison."

When even church ministers were starting to support their cause, the WSPU felt vindicated in their approach. They were about, however, to embark on an even more violent campaign of militant suffrage, one which would cost them a great deal of public support – but with hindsight, it must be questioned whether, without such militant behaviour, the women's movement would have moved on at the pace it did? The campaign that was about to ensue lost them several prominent supporters, including George Bernard Shaw, the man who had previously said that women should do all they could to secure the vote, including maiming and killing. He had, however, had a change of heart. In September 1912, he wrote about the two women who had set fire to a theatre in Dublin, Mary

Leigh and Gladys Evans, now in prison in Dublin on hunger strike and enduring force-feeding. They had been sentenced to five years of penal servitude. A petition had been set up in protest at their treatment, and Bernard Shaw wrote an open letter to Miss Gawthorpe, the woman who was organizing the petition. Most people expected it would be in support of her cause, but his words came as a shock:

> *"Until the Dublin incident the offences for which Suffragists were imprisoned were so trivial that nobody seriously believed that women should be severely punished for them.... But the Dublin incident was not trivial. To set fire to a theatre is beyond all question a serious crime. If the suffragists may commit arson with impunity ... then they may assassinate, throw express trains off the line, blow up the Houses of Parliament with dynamite or, in short, do anything mischievous and murderous. This is an impunity which no community will stand; and women who are prepared to go to such lengths must clearly be restrained in some way. I do not say that they should be punished, because I do not believe that anybody should be punished; but restrained they certainly must be, just as necessarily as a tiger must be restrained." (14 September 1912)*

George Bernard Shaw was not the only former supporter of the militant suffragettes who felt their behaviour had gone too far. The feminist writer Rebecca West, who had long been a supporter of the Pankhursts, and who had written intelligently scathing articles about Mrs Humphry Ward and her anti-suffrage crusade, was disappointed by the turn the militants had taken. She described the Pankhursts and their supporters as carrying out "a programme of massive vandalism". She felt that the position they were taking was foolish, as it would isolate them politically and socially and would put the movement back rather than carrying it forward.

The Conciliation Bill, the ignoring of which had renewed the WSPU's fervour for militancy, was not perfect – in fact, had it been passed, very few women would have been granted the vote – but it would have been the first stage on the road to full equality. Two more Conciliation Bills were drawn up, one in 1911 and another in 1912, but despite majority backing from MPs of all parties, these bills were blocked by Asquith. In 1913, the NUWSS sent out a press release explaining what was happening and how deceitful they believed Asquith to be:

"In May, 1908, Mr. Asquith replied to a deputation of Liberal members of Parliament that he intended to introduce, during the lifetime of that Parliament, an effective electoral reform, and it would clearly be within the competence of those present to introduce by amendments or by extensions the object they desire. Such amendments the Government would not oppose.

In December, 1909, on the eve of the General Election, Mr. Asquith repeated this promise to the Women's Liberal Federation, stating that it would still hold good in the next Parliament.

In June, 1910, the Conciliation Bill, drafted by a committee of suffragist members of all parties, was introduced and passed by a majority of 110. Mr. Asquith refused facilities for carrying this Bill into law on the ground that it was not capable of free amendment.

In May, 1911, the Conciliation Bill, altered so as to be capable of free amendment, was again introduced, and passed its second reading by a majority of 167.

Facilities were again asked and again refused, but an offer was made of facilities in 1912 when the Bill had again been read a second time.

*On the strength of this promise the suffragists throughout
the country worked indefatigably to secure a majority for
the Bill through all its stages, and success seemed assured
when in November, 1911, Mr. Asquith announced his
intention of introducing a Reform Bill which would
enfranchise practically every man and no woman."*

Following Black Friday, members of the WSPU targeted Asquith
himself, yelling abuse and smashing windows at his home and,
memorably, the windows of a cab in which he had taken shelter from
the mob of women in Downing Street. Other MPs' homes were also
targeted and those unfortunate enough to be on Downing Street
in the week following Black Friday found themselves kicked and
pummelled by a 400-strong mob of furious suffragettes, meting out
the same treatment that they had received at the hands of police and
anti-suffrage men the week before. The police were reportedly taken
by surprise at the strength and fury of the women and were caught
so off-guard that the protestors were able to make their way halfway
up Downing Street before the police managed to take back control,
by which point a couple of missiles had been hurled at 10 Downing
Street. Neither of them hit the window panes, but one furrowed an
indentation into the wall. On that day, 22 November 1910, even more
arrests took place than on Black Friday; over 150 people were arrested
and this time Churchill showed no leniency. The newspapers blamed
him for the violence, naively stating that if he had sent all the Black
Friday protesters to prison then the suffragettes would have been so
cowed that the second demonstration would not have taken place.[10]

---

10. This was not the only top story in the newspapers at the time. On the
same pages as the reports of Black Friday and the Downing Street protest
were articles about Dr Hawley Crippen, who was to be hanged on 23
November 1910 for the murder of his wife Cora. While the suffragettes
were protesting about the Conciliation Bill, supporters of Dr Crippen
were putting together a petition of over 15,000 signatures from people
who believed him innocent.

Chapter Seventeen

"The amount of opposition with which the advocates of women's rights have had to contend would have killed any movement, had that movement not been founded upon an unshakable moral idealism.... For men to hold in their hands the fortunes and lives of women is a mockery and denial of liberty. Democracy knows no sex."

Ronald H. Kidd, *For Freedom's Cause, An Appeal to Working Men*, 1912 (WSPU publication)

With the start of a new decade, there was a despondent feeling that the women's suffrage movement was going to fail, that those women who had fought so hard for the vote might never see it within their lifetime. The women recognized that the Conservatives were unlikely to give them the vote if they got back into power, but what had seemed like such a promise of success from the Liberal government had also come to nothing. For many in Britain, 1910 had been a year of sadness with the death of King Edward VII, who had waited for so many decades to succeed his mother and who had, against all Queen Victoria's dire predictions of incompetence, proved a popular king. Edward was succeeded by his son, King George V, and Queen Mary. Unfortunately Queen Mary was a known supporter of the anti-suffrage movement, and for the first few years of their reign she forbade any of her ladies-in-waiting from being involved with the suffrage movement. (She did not lift the ban until 1914.)

Determined to show their loyalty to their new monarchs, a variety of suffrage societies joined together for the Suffrage Coronation Procession on 17 June 1911. The photographer Christina Broom, from Fulham in south London, photographed many of the different groups and produced commemorative portraits. This was a non-militant event. Women were encouraged to wear their finest clothes and to behave with regal decorum, showing the general public that suffragists were not "unsexed", wild creatures but elegant, intelligent women. It was estimated that 40,000 women took part in the procession, not only from all over Britain but also from different parts of the British Empire. Every society brought proudly hand-made banners; there were floats, and bands playing music, and many attendees wore fancy dress to show the importance of women throughout Britain's history. Composer Ethel Smyth[1] wrote "March of the Women" for the Coronation Procession, and dedicated it to Emmeline Pankhurst.

The lyrics included the verse:

"Long, long – we in the past
Cowered in dread from the light of heaven,
Strong, strong – stand we at last,
Fearless in faith and with sight new given.
Strength with its beauty, Life with its duty,
(Hear the voice, oh hear and obey!)
These, these – beckon us on!
Open your eyes to the blaze of the day."

---

1. When interviewed by Dame Vera Brittain in 1937 for the National Programme on BBC radio, Ethel Smyth remembered her friend Emmeline Pankhurst standing in Smyth's garden, trying to learn how to throw stones accurately so as to be able to target individual windows at demonstrations. Smyth commented wryly, "Mrs Pankhurst was no cricketer."

Mr Reginald Potts had also written a special marching song for the WSPU, "The Purple, White and Green March", which included the words:

"Purple stands for the loyal heart,
Loyal to cause and King;
White for Purity, Green for hope,
Bright hopes of Spring.
March and fight through the long, long night
That our children be brave and free!
March and fight for our one common right,
Citizens to be!"

Throughout much of 1911, the suffrage movement carried out peaceful protests, the most famous of which was the refusal to take part in the census. The boycott was heralded by the phrase "Women do not count, neither shall they be counted". When it came to census day, on 2 April 2011, suffrage campaigners played an elaborate game of hide and seek with the census workers, avoiding being counted in the census return either at their own homes or elsewhere. In the same year, two books were published by suffrage leaders: Millicent Garrett Fawcett's *Women's Suffrage* and Sylvia Pankhurst's *The Suffragette*.

Throughout the country, women and their families were making changes and their own personal protests. Newspapers reported with astonishment a "suffragette wedding" in London, in January 1912, at which the bride's father did not "give her away" and at which the bride did not want to say the word "obey" in her marriage vows. The tone of several of the newspaper reports seemed to suggest that both the bride's father and the groom must have been crazy to allow such behaviour. The story was reported as far afield as Scotland, where the *Dundee Courier* announced that the officiating priest, Rev. Hugh Chapman, had been advised that the "legality of the wedding" might be in question if the wording of the vows was changed, so "obey" was kept in, but reportedly repeated with derision. Both the bride, Una Stratford Dugdale, and the groom, Victor Duval, were prominent in the WSPU. The wedding guests included Lady Constance Lytton, Christabel Pankhurst and the Pethick-Lawrences.

The WSPU had been deliberately keeping the peace while the second version of the Conciliation Bill was presented to MPs, but they had been waiting for the call to return to arms. At a WSPU meeting at the Steinway Hall in London, at the start of 1911, the suffragette Mrs Pertwee declared: "...one thing is certain and that is that we shall not be gagged. Women are ready to march in battalions on this crusade for liberty and justice. Now is the time to work, we have a majority of 264 in the House in our favour, and every hand should be at the wheel and there should be no slackness."[2] When the Pankhursts realized that, once again, Asquith's government not only had no intention of passing the Bill – despite it being approved by a majority of MPs a second time – and was now considering a Bill that would give votes to even more men and yet still none to women, there was a call to action. In response to Asquith's announcement, the window smashers went out in force and smashed "hundreds" of windows all over the country.

The return to militancy saw an explosion of pent-up fury, with suffragettes tired of being duped by male politicians and harassed by the police. Their months of peaceful protest had made absolutely no difference to the position of women, so it was decided that it was time to return to more aggressive tactics. Added to which, the anti-suffrage movement had been growing increasingly vocal. In 1910, the Anti-Suffrage League boasted 16,000 members around the country and a reported 400,000 people had signed a petition opposing women's suffrage.[3] In February 1912, the Liberal MP for East Bristol, Charles Hobhouse, made a speech that the Pankhursts and their followers saw as incitement to further militancy. At the Colston Hall in Bristol,

---

2. The speech was recorded by an observer for the Metropolitan Police, 23 February 1911 (the transcript is now in the National Archives at Kew).

3. Figures from Warwick University archives.

Hobhouse told the crowds that the issue of female suffrage had not inspired any "popular sentimental uprising" or any "great ebulition of popular feeling". Emmeline Pankhurst responded by telling her followers that Hobhouse's speech deserved a militant reaction and the suffragettes acted on her words by attacking buildings, and people, throughout Bristol. The activities of the WSPU had changed radically since *Votes for Women* had reported on a "militant" action in 1908:

> *"At 11 o'clock on Saturday morning, just when the streets were crowded with people and traffic, Mrs Annot Robinson, Miss Capper and Miss Marsden mounted the steps of the Queen Victoria Memorial Statue ... and displayed on the base of the statue a large card bearing the motto of the Union on a banneret decorated with iris lilies.... Several policemen made their way through the large crowd ... and ordered the removal of the placards. As they had to admit that floral tributes were not forbidden, Mrs Robinson slowly plucked the flowers one by one from the card and laid them on the pedestal. By this time their main object was achieved, for the pressmen and photographers were on the spot."*

Militancy had changed beyond recognition since the slow placing of flowers on a pedestal had been considered a "militant" occurrence.

In the same month as Hobhouse made his ill-received speech, Christabel called on the Labour party, which was slowly growing in influence, to vote against the Liberal party at every turn until women had secured the vote. When the Labour party refused to agree to her demands, she began what she called a "war" on the Labour party.

The WSPU's militant tactics were giving the union the reputation of a terrorist organization and the government began to respond accordingly. On 1 and 4 March 1912, two outbreaks of window smashing took place in the West End of London. Nearly 200 women were arrested and many sent to prison. Amongst those who ended up in Holloway was the well-respected composer Ethel Smyth. She was visited in her cell by the famous conductor Sir Thomas Beecham, who related that, while he was visiting, Smyth had heard the suffragettes out in the exercise yard singing her "March of the Women". She leant out of her tiny cell window and conducted the singers below, substituting her well-worn toothbrush for a conductor's baton.

In the same month as the window-smashing protests, the police raided the home of the Pethick-Lawrences, the WSPU headquarters. Emmeline and Frederick Pethick-Lawrence were arrested – but Christabel, having received a tip-off before the raid, was nowhere to be seen. Although Emmeline Pankhurst was famed for being imprisoned and for her constant hunger strikes, her daughter (who together with Annie Kenney had been the first of the suffragettes to be imprisoned) now chose to avoid imprisonment. Her publicity stunt was to disappear. It was extremely effective. The first that the general public knew of her disappearance was in reports of the trial of those who had been arrested at the WSPU office and elsewhere that day. The newspapers reported mysteriously, "Miss Christabel Pankhurst was not in custody," "Miss Pankhurst was not present," and "Miss Pankhurst had not been arrested before the opening of the Court."

Soon the news broke that she had escaped and that Scotland Yard was baffled: it was reported that "an extensive search has been made in London and elsewhere", but Christabel's hiding place remained a mystery. To the newspaper-reading public, Christabel took on something of a Scarlet Pimpernel persona, with newspapers full of sensationalist headlines such as "Where is Christabel?", "Suffrage Leader Still At Large" and "Miss Pankhurst Eludes the Police". Suffragette meetings were interrupted by curious bystanders calling out to the speakers to reveal Christabel's hiding place, and imprisoned suffrage leaders were interrogated as to her whereabouts. It was reported that there was a police guard still at the WSPU offices, should she return, and that a watch was being kept on the homes of friends she might contact.

Many WSPU members seemed to be as baffled as the police. Eventually, when it was realized that this was no mere publicity stunt and Christabel had genuinely fled, the mood changed and comments started to be made that she was a traitor who should have given herself up in support of her comrades. An unnamed WSPU spokeswoman was provoked to declare, "Although we are without news of her whereabouts, we feel that she is acting in the best interests of the movement, whatever her plans may be." Despite the bravado and support when members were interviewed by the press, there were nonetheless whispers within the WSPU that Christabel had abandoned her followers to their fate but was not willing to sacrifice herself in the way she had asked others to do.

With Christabel on the run and Emmeline Pankhurst reported to be suffering from bronchitis in prison, suffragettes around the country continued to keep the battles going. In March 1912, one weary-sounding journalist reported that yet "more batches of suffragettes" had been arrested for window smashing. A surprised Glaswegian journalist wrote about the arrest of "a well-dressed lady suffragette" who had smashed six windows at one of the city's prestigious shops. Anti-suffrage women began to gather in groups and harass lone suffragettes selling *Votes for Women* on the streets and to heckle speakers at outdoor meetings.

Thrilling stories of where the elusive Christabel might be, akin to those from a spy novel, appeared in newspapers, as did suggestions of how the renegade suffragette could be captured. The London *Evening Standard* printed the following account on 7 March 1912: "At one time Scotland Yard was on a hot scent. The information came to them that Miss Pankhurst was in the house of a friend, and was actually keeping in touch with her office by telephone! Would she dare? For a short time the telephone was 'tapped' by the sleuths in plain clothes."

When *Votes for Women* repeated the *Standard* story, the allegation of "phone tapping" was denied vigorously by Scotland Yard.

At the end of March 1912, a message from Christabel was sent from her hiding place and read out at a WSPU meeting: "My very heart and soul are with you.... The Government had struck us a hard blow, and we rise stronger and more triumphant than ever because of their attack.... Our spirit is strengthened and our hearts are lifted higher by everything done with intent to intimidate us.... They will tear the stars from the sky before they break the spirit of women in this country."

Christabel was spotted all over the country, from Reigate in Surrey to Auchterarder in Perthshire, as well as further afield. A passenger on board the ship *Mauretania* informed the authorities that he had definitely seen Christabel on board and that she must now be on the run in America. Rumours also began to emerge that Christabel had fled to Paris, where an "informant" had purportedly recognized her walking along a boulevard. She was also identified at a "French watering place". A telegram from Boston to the newspapers claimed that Christabel had now left but that she had been in Massachusetts, staying at the home of an Englishwoman who ran the Sherborne Prison. One London newspaper boy made the papers himself when he played a practical joke on passers-by. He had been given two newspaper billboards relating to the day's big stories: Christabel's disappearance and an expedition to Antarctica. He tore the two bills in half and placed them next to each other so that his newsstand read "Miss Christabel Pankhurst At the South Pole". *Votes for Women* reported a story in which they claimed police had raided the house of a woman after she had sent a postcard to a friend on which was written "I am afraid I shall have to get rid of Christabel Pankhurst, her temper has got so very bad. I suppose it is from being shut up so much". The paper alleged that three detectives had turned up at her home whereupon they encountered a lapdog named after the missing suffragette leader.

In September, *Votes for Women* announced that Christabel was indeed living in Paris. She spoke French well and had relatives living nearby, so she had taken up residence in the city, from where she had continued to direct WSPU operations from the very beginning of her disappearance. Following her release from prison, Emmeline Pankhurst had joined her daughter, who was nursing her back to health. The announcement of where Christabel was living was made after it had been established that, because she was a political refugee, she could not be arrested by the British police in France. From the moment her whereabouts were known, foreign correspondents based in Paris released interviews with her to papers all over the world – it was not only the British newspapers that had become fascinated by Christabel. On 14 September 1912, a small local newspaper in America, *The Pittsburgh Press*, reported her story with all the glee of a thrilling mystery novel:

> *"Miss Christabel Pankhurst arrived in Paris from a small fishing village near Calais, having long ago eluded the London police who wanted her for sufraget [sic] outrages. 'I left London as soon as the raid last March was over,' she said. 'It was not difficult to evade the police. I did not disguise myself; I simply discarded the green costume and veil that are the uniform of our union. I went straight to the French coast, where I spent the summer.... I received many visits. My mother always kept in touch with my movements and sent weekly letters and our paper. I met several who recognized me, but they kept my secret. I shall now stay in Paris, and continue my work.*
>
> *'I have investigated the matter and find that England cannot touch me, as my offense does not come under the extradition treaty. Anyway, it would be absurd for England, whose traditional policy it is to shelter political refugees, to interfere with those in other countries.*
>
> *'Till we get the vote we shall continue our present methods. We can do so. We are all well and strong, and the battle is invigorating.'"*

The Paris correspondent for the *Daily Chronicle* was one of the first to interview her and to reveal that she had travelled to France under the pseudonym of "Miss Parker". In an article entitled "The Adventures of Christabel", the suffrage leader explained that the WSPU had anticipated the police raid on the offices at Clement's Inn, which is why she was not at the office when the arrests were made:

> "When the warning of danger reached her she set off to France without delay. Taking a motor-bus to Charing-Cross Station she caught the afternoon Continental train, and travelled quite openly and without any attempt at concealment. When approaching the Channel steamer's gangway she felt somewhat nervous, but on the steamer no one paid any particular attention to the trim figure of the unaccompanied English girl wearing a brown travelling coat and motoring cap."
> (Daily Chronicle, 12 September 1912)

Christabel was usually described in terms of a woman of fashion – often with wonderment that such a militant suffragette still took such good care of herself when it came to personal appearance. In March 1912, the *Cheltenham Onlooker* wrote an article about Christabel in which her suffragette activities seem to be secondary to the comment that "Miss Pankhurst is essentially womanly in all things, and a favourite even with those who do not share her political views". This description was typical of the manner in which Christabel was written about. She and her mother made the most of their looks and insisted that if they were to win the nation over, suffragettes should always strive to be the best-dressed, most alluring women at any social gathering. In pro-suffrage newspapers, favourable reports arrived from Paris, where Christabel was said to be extremely popular and receiving praise for her great skill as an orator. Christabel was written about in the style in which today's "celebrity" magazines write about TV personalities, sometimes contemptuous and seemingly scornful but nonetheless fully aware of how mention even of the smallest minutiae of her life sold newspapers. In December 1913, the *Evening Telegraph* devoted a column to the safe return home of Christabel's dog: "Miss

Christabel Pankhurst's pomeranian dog has returned to its home. The pom is called Wspu – pronounced in one syllable. However Wspu has returned. She – for, of course, she is a she – was found near Luna Park [Paris] the other evening by an Englishwoman, who returned it to the address upon the collar, and once again Christabel was happy."

In the autumn of 1913, Emmeline Pankhurst made the newspapers in America. She had travelled to New York in order to address suffrage meetings, but found herself detained under the "moral turpitude clause" and about to be deported. While she was kept at Ellis Island, she was visited by the American suffrage leader Mrs Harriet Stanton Blatch and a group of supporters. The *New York Times* reported:

> "Mrs Emmeline Pankhurst ... repeated her threat to start a 'hunger strike' if barred from this country. 'If I am deported from this city I shall be dead 24 hours after sailing, because I am too weak to stand the strain,' she said.... When [her visitors] arrived at her rooms Mrs Pankhurst was found garbed in a gray flowered silk kimono, taking nourishment in the shape of grapes, pears, and bananas with buttered toast and tea. She greeted her visitors cordially and after kissing them said that she had found the mattress an excellent one and had slept well. 'I am a prisoner, don't forget that,' said Mrs Pankhurst, pointing to the nurses who kept passing in and out of her room. 'These good ladies must obey orders, and come in to see that I am still here.'"

In response to the accusations of "moral turpitude", Emmeline Pankhurst responded that the ancestors of every American could be accused of the same thing. She was released and allowed to start her tour. As usual, in her remarkably astute way, she had managed to turn around the problems she had encountered and use them as superb publicity. Her speech at Madison Square Gardens was delivered the day after she had received Harriet Stanton Blatch in her room on Ellis Island and was reported in all the papers. Mrs Pankhurst also received a telegram of support from one of the most influential female campaigners in America, Jane Addams from Chicago. In it, Addams called upon America to "shelter" the British suffragette in the same way that "our sister republic, France" was sheltering Christabel Pankhurst.

In London, and within the WSPU, however, the big scandal of the year was that Emmeline and Frederick Pethick-Lawrence, despite their years not only of loyalty and hard work but of bankrolling the union, as well as their months of imprisonment while Christabel was safely in Paris, had been unceremoniously expelled from the WSPU. Their crime had been to criticize the increasing violence of Emmeline and Christabel Pankhurst's actions and speeches. With the departure of the Pethick-Lawrences, the WSPU also lost the journal *Votes for Women*, which the couple had masterminded and edited (as well as supported financially).

Christabel set up a new WSPU journal, entitled simply *The Suffragette*. Emmeline Pankhurst was in full support of her daughter's more militant approach, sickened by what she perceived as the duplicity of the politicians and the general apathy among the population. In October of 1912, she had opened a suffragettes' meeting at London's Royal Albert Hall with the words "I incite this meeting to rebellion".

The result of Emmeline Pankhurst's exhortation was a marked increase in militant suffrage alongside an increase in hostile newspaper reporting. Public – and editorial – opinion might have started to show sympathy towards the suffragettes following Black Friday, but with the upsurge of suffragette "hooliganism", the tide took a determined turn away from public sympathy. Now the newspapers were full of words such as "insanity", "madness" and "hysteria"[4] – that

---

4. The Greek word hustera translates to "womb". Ancient Graeco-Roman medical men attributed the condition they named hysteria to being caused by a woman's womb "moving" in a violent manner – for centuries, the womb was believed to be able to travel around the body – and causing emotional and physical upheaval. Hysteria was therefore perceived as a uniquely female malady.

malady of women caused, according to the word's ancient Greek root, by the possession of a womb and which made certain male medics claim women were constitutionally unstable and therefore inferior to men. It was discovered that imprisoned suffragettes were being "medically examined" on the orders of the government, in an attempt to have them all declared insane; the government was also accused of drugging the women in order to make them more compliant to force-feeding. Despite the brutality, the women were determined. Suffragette Kitty Marion was recorded as having endured force-feeding more than 200 times.

By the start of 1913, suffragists and suffragettes alike were receiving short shrift in the newspapers, with headlines such as "Wild Scenes in Wales" and "The Militants' Madness" above articles containing phrases such as "those mad creatures", "this tyranny of organized blackguardism" and "the excesses which a gang of politico-mad women can perpetrate". Even when the deeds committed amounted to petty, witty vandalism rather than violent attacks, journalists wrote about them in furious language. In 1912, the newspapers had declared themselves outraged at what was probably the least violent and most amusing of the recent suffragette actions. Suffragettes were reported to have "invaded" the grounds at the royal residence of Balmoral in Scotland. They had, however, committed no acts of violence; instead they had simply removed all the coloured flags on the royal golf course, replacing them with flags in the suffragette colours.

In February 1913, suffragettes targeted the Royal St George's Golf Club in Sandwich, Kent. Armed with trowels, the women scooped out little holes all over the course and inserted into the holes pieces of paper bearing the words "Votes for Women". At other courses around the country women left similar messages, as well as messages inside glass bottles bearing the legend "No votes, no golf". They also buried suffragette banners in the sand in bunkers, ready to be discovered by unsuspecting players.

These petty acts of vandalism, however, were eclipsed by the very serious actions, such as that which George Bernard Shaw had railed against in Dublin. Many suffragettes had turned to much more dangerous crimes, including arson and bomb-making. On 19 February 1913, the Surrey police were alerted to the news that an explosion had taken place at a house in Walton-on-the-Hill, shortly after 6am. The property was in the process of being renovated for David Lloyd George. Luckily for the developer, several of the home-made bombs did not detonate and the damage was far less extensive than it could have been. The attack was carried out when the house was empty and before the builders arrived at work for the day – but the papers were quick to point out that, had all the bombs functioned, they could well have exploded after the workmen arrived. Astonishment was expressed that Emmeline Pankhurst not only took responsibility for her supporters' actions but praised them for the violence. As the newspapers reported, she "declared with brutal frankness, 'We have blown up the house of the Chancellor of the Exchequer … I personally accept full responsibility for it.'" She said the attack had been carried out to "wake up" Lloyd George from an anti-suffrage lethargy. A month later, another large house in Surrey, in the village of Englefield Green, was targeted: it was called Trevethan and owned by Lady White. The house had been empty for over three years, so no one was injured, but the damage was extensive and estimates for the repairs were reported to be anything from £2,000 to £5,000 (depending on which newspaper report can be believed). A local policeman recalled having seen two women pass by on bicycles not long before the explosion. One of the notes left behind at the scene said: "Stop torturing our comrades in prison."

On 31 January 1913, the *Morning Post* reported from a WSPU meeting a speech by Annie Kenney:

> *"Speaking of militant tactics, she said she would like to see a sandwich board procession marching through London with the words 'Wanted, more Window Smashers'. No woman ought to go out without a hammer in her pocket. Let the women who could not break windows do something else. They could all do the pillar-boxes. But do not let them be too keen and get arrested. It was their*

duty to create a situation. They wished to see the British Museum and the National Gallery closed and all the shops barricaded. Let them make it like a siege. Everyone could do some little thing to make public life intolerable. The thing was to be militant."

As Annie Kenney's speech makes explicit, for the WSPU this was no longer merely a protest, it was all-out war. In February 1913, the *Morning Post* reported on the arsenal of weapons discovered at the studio of an artist and suffragette in Notting Hill, West London. The 32-year-old woman was discovered to have "corrosive fluid, clippers for cutting telegraph wires, fire lighters, hammers, flints ... [and] a number of false motor-car identification plates". All over the country, churches (because the Church of England as an institution supported the government, and church teachings were seen as oppressive towards women), train stations, bridges and other public buildings were targeted, set on fire and, in the most frightening cases, booby-trapped with bombs. The *Derby Daily Telegraph* reported: "Owing to suffragette outrages in various parts of the country, Chatsworth House and Haddon Hall are being specially guarded night and day by police and gamekeepers" (5 April 1913). Guards were also on the alert at art galleries all over the country after paintings were slashed by WSPU militants at Manchester Art Gallery.

The police had their new weapons of war. The National Archives in Kew contains records of the methods used, including boxes of covert photographs taken with a "spy camera" or a Ross Telecentric camera lens. The long lens allowed the police to carry out secret photographic surveillance, keeping a record of the women they suspected of carrying out crimes. The spy camera allowed the police to photograph suffragettes at demonstrations, meetings and outside their homes. One of the protests that women undertook was the refusal to be photographed in prison; these women were often held down and forced to keep still long enough to be photographed. One suffragette was restrained by being held around the neck by a prison warder's arm; the photographer then "touched up" the image, so that instead of the viewer being able to see an arm, it looked as though the prisoner was wearing a scarf.

With the return of militancy, many people who had previously supported the suffragettes now thought that their actions were going too far. This was made explicit when the Royal Albert Hall notified the WSPU to say that they were no longer welcome to hire the hall for suffragette meetings.

Incensed by how the suffragettes' activities were impacting on everyday life, people began to fight back. Newspapers reported that crowds were turning out in force to disrupt suffrage meetings, using the same tactics that the suffragettes used to disrupt political rallies, church services and council meetings. When it was known that there was to be a suffrage event, local people would bar the way of the women or throw eggs at the speakers. The newspapers reported on one such occurrence in Wimbledon in the spring of 1913:

> "Before the meeting on Wimbledon Common was timed to commence several thousand people had assembled, and the police were present in strong force. As soon as the meeting was opened the crowd started booing, and the singing of hymns, comic songs, and ragtime tunes drowned the speakers' voices. The police forced back the crowd, and formed a strong cordon round the speakers. The shouting and singing continued, and the speakers failing to obtain a hearing, the meeting terminated abruptly, the Suffragettes being escorted away by mounted police."

In May 1913, an "explosive machine" was discovered secreted inside St Paul's cathedral, wrapped up in pages from a recent copy of *The Suffragette*. The bomb did not explode and was removed without causing any damage. An expert from the Royal Engineers pronounced that "the mechanism had apparently failed to work". That incident and the burning down of a tea-room and the "wanton destruction" of valuable orchids at Kew Gardens provoked fury as striking not at the government but at the unwitting public.

Communications were damaged by suffragettes cutting telegraph wires and railway-signal wires, and destroying letters – the practice of dropping vials of phosphorus into post-boxes led unsuspecting postal workers to suffer terrible burns on their hands when they collected the letters (which were also damaged). Militant violence was no longer aimed only at the government: anyone who happened to be walking past, visiting or working in one of the targeted buildings was at risk. People were living in fear of being targeted in an act of violence just for being in the wrong place at the wrong time. The public was outraged and there was a general clamour for the suffragettes to be locked up.

One of the main reasons that WSPU actions were so often able to evade detection was because of the large funds at the union's disposal. In 1913, the Commissioner of the Metropolitan Police wrote a frustrated letter to the Secretary of State about how so many militant suffragettes were managing to escape arrest:

> "I have to acquaint you … that the members of the Women's Social and Political Union have at their disposal two Motor Cars which they are known to employ in connection with their numerous acts or attempted acts of incendiarism, also for the purpose of escaping arrest; and the duty of keeping Police observation on these Motor Cars is frequently impossible to perform owing to the fact that when outside the town they travel too fast for any conveyance at the disposal of the police to keep up with them.

> "It is thought that this difficulty might be met by the employment of a Police Officer on a Motor Bicycle and that the cost of a machine suitable for the purpose would be £55 to £70."[5]

---

5. Written from New Scotland Yard, 20 October 1913, now held in the National Archives at Kew. The motorcyclist failed on more than one occasion because his vehicle did not have an automatic starter motor.

Public pressure was mounting on the government to do something to punish the suffragettes, yet at the same time the furore over prison brutality and force-feeding in particular was still raging. In April 1913, the government introduced the Cat and Mouse Act.[6] The act's correct name was the "Prisoners' Temporary Discharge for Ill-Health Act", described as "An Act to provide for the Temporary Discharge of Prisoners whose further detention in prison is undesirable on account of the condition of their Health". The act allowed for prisoners on hunger strike to be released when they became too weak or ill through lack of food to be kept safely in prison. This release was only temporary: once they had been nursed back to health, they would be returned to prison to continue their sentence to the end. Emmeline Pankhurst was jailed and released 11 times. The act was rushed through Parliament as a desperate measure to deal with all the adverse publicity garnered by the practice of force-feeding. The terms of the act included the clause (ironically, as was standard legal procedure, referring to the prisoner as "he"):

"Any prisoner so discharged shall comply with any conditions stated in the order of the temporary discharge, and shall return to prison at the expiration of the period stated in the order, or of such extended period as may be fixed by any subsequent order of the Secretary of State, and, if the prisoner fails to comply of return, he may be arrested without warrant and taken back to prison."

---

6. Also passed that year was the Mental Deficiency Act, drafted in consultation with leading eugenicists. Winston Churchill was particularly interested in the practice that had been recommended to him of introducing compulsory sterilization for anyone declared mentally ill. One of the categories being considered was "sexually feeble-minded", meaning that promiscuous women could have been labelled "mentally deficient" and criminalized. That particular category was removed at the draft stage, but the new act did allow frightening legislation over pauper women who gave birth to illegitimate children.

Members of the Matchmakers Union, 1888, who went on strike at the Bryant and May's factory in London.

Annie Besant (1847–1933), in 1895. The English theosophist, who was prominent in the Fabian Society, published a pamphlet on birth control for which she was brought to trial on a charge of obscenity. She moved to India where she lectured and became the Hindu nationalist leader.

Suffragist leader Lady Emmeline Pethick-Lawrence (1868–1954) celebrates her release in 1909.

The suffragist Annie Kenney (1879–1953) is arrested during a demonstration in 1913.

Mary Arnold Ward, also known as Mrs Humphry Ward, portrait, (1851–1920). She was born in Tasmania but came to England at the age of five. She became a novelist and a writer of serious didactic books as an opponent of women's emancipation.

The British suffragette leader Emmeline Pankhurst (1858–1928), and her daughter Christabel (1880–1958), founders of the Women's Social and Political Union, wearing prison uniforms during a spell in jail in 1908 for demonstrating for women's rights.

Emmeline Pankhurst is arrested at a demonstration outside Buckingham Palace, London, 1914.

Enormous crowds of women thronged Victoria Embankment in 1915, despite a drizzling rain, to participate in the women's procession voicing the demand that the British Government use women in the work of making ammunition, replacing the men. It is estimated that 50,000 women were in the procession which was led by Mrs Emmeline Pankhurst (third from left, front row). With the demonstrators were also a number of titled women including Lady Colebrook, Lady Knollys and Mrs Waldorf Astor.

The "Pank-a-Squith" board game dates from 1909 and was produced by the WSPU who were notable for their use of marketing and humour.

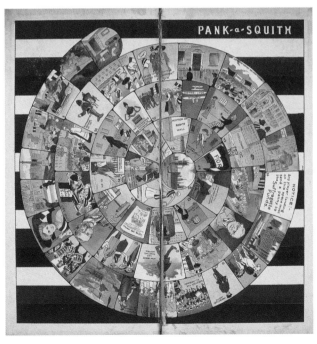

Above, left: The British feminist and suffragist Millicent Fawcett (1847–1929), circa 1870.

Above, right: Policemen arrest Suffragettes who had chained themselves to the railings of Buckingham Palace.

Elizabeth Garrett Anderson (1836–1917) was the first woman doctor in England. Anderson had become a nurse at Middlesex Hospital, London, after being refused entry at several medical schools because she was a woman. However, she later discovered that the Society of Apothecaries did not specify that women were banned from taking examinations, and in 1865 she passed their examination to become a doctor.

A handbill advertising the Women's Coronation Procession on Saturday 17 June, 1911. A suffragette is taking part in a "poster parade". Her sandwich board is advertising the procession and the handbill gives details of the "monster" rally to be held afterwards, with speakers including Christabel and Emmeline Pankhurst. The bill was printed in the suffragette colours of purple, green and white.

Emily Wilding Davison (1872–1913) is trampled beneath King George V's horse, Anmer, during the Derby at the Epsom Race Course in 1913.

The American-born British politician Nancy Witcher Langhorne, Viscountess Astor (1879–1964), at the declaration of the poll in Plymouth. She became the first woman member of parliament.

The National Women's Party
of the USA takes part in a
procession demonstrating in
favour of an equal franchise for
UK men and women in London,
July 1926.

Two sophisticated and
fashionable ladies in heels,
cloche hats and fur-trimmed
coats alight from a taxi at a
polling station where they will
vote for the first time in the
General Election of May 1929.

Just as the general public had read with glee about Christabel Pankhurst's escape from the police, the papers reported about suffragette "mice" who managed to elude the police after being released early from prison. One of the most famous was Lilian Lenton, who had been found guilty of the arson attack on Kew Gardens. Under the title "Dramatic Arrest of a Mouse", the *Evening News* reported on 5 May 1914:

> "Lilian Lenton, authoress of the best-laid plans of the Suffragette 'mice' for baffling the police, has been caught once more ... the house to which she was removed was watched, but once again the elusive Lilian did the vanishing trick – with complete success – dressed as a young man.
>
> She went on another motor tour, and led the police a merry dance up and down the country for several weeks while she changed her disguises. Harrogate, Scarborough, and Dundee were a few of the towns she visited.
>
> She also stayed at Cardiff. There she was nearly caught, but by disguising herself as an infirm old lady, with a black shawl over her head, she hobbled into the station and travelled to London."

The suffrage societies were appalled at the callousness of the Cat and Mouse Act and the unpleasantness of the language that accompanied it. Millicent Garrett Fawcett lobbied MPs, but the government stayed firm. In 1912, her friend, the pro-suffrage MP Lord Robert Cecil, had written an article for the *Daily Graphic* in which he had tried to defend the reasons for militancy:

> "The women believe, with too much reason, that their demands are set aside by the chicanery of politicians,

*without regard to the authority of the people.... For this
evil what is the remedy? How can we restore confidence
in government? Only by making our Constitution accord
with the facts of the situation. The only claim of the House
of Commons to its place in our Constitution is that it
represents the people. But does it? No one really thinks so."*
("Parliament and People", Daily Graphic, 14 May 1912)

A year later, however, the militancy had become so violent that Cecil
was no longer able to defend the suffragettes' actions despite his own
horror at the Cat and Mouse Act and the feelings it had engendered.
He wrote a letter to Millicent in which he conveyed his sadness at the
bitterness of the warfare between the WSPU and MPs:

25 July 1913
Dear Mrs Fawcett,

*I am sorry your interview with Bonar Law was so
unsatisfactory – but I fear it is true that so long as militancy
goes on nothing can be done with the Conservatives. This
is very unfair but it is also very characteristic of the male
political mind. I was shocked at the kind of Wild Beast
feeling displayed in the House during our little Cat and
Mouse Debate on Wednesday and I found the Hereford
people – where I have just been – fully as bad!*

Yours very truly,
Robert Cecil[7]

---

7. This letter can be seen in the collection at the Women's Library in
London.

Christabel was also causing a furore with her articles, despatched from Paris for *The Suffragette*. In September 1913, *The Evening Standard* called her journalism an "appeal to indecency" as Christabel was writing not only about militant politics but also about the role of women in society in general and how it needed to change, calling upon women to empower themselves in all areas of their lives:

"From the security of her Paris refuge this fugitive from justice has ... been dealing with what has been called the 'secret scourge' [venereal disease] in a more outspoken manner than even a medical man would adopt in professional journals.... It is no exaggeration to say that the half dozen articles on 'Chastity in Men' and 'The Dangers of Marriage' are the most daringly indecent matter published within our memory. They deal with questions which should never be discussed except between a doctor and his patient, and they are extraordinarily suggestive to young men and women who constitute the principal part of the readers of The Suffragette. It is a scandal that such publications should be on public sale, and it is undoubtedly the duty of the authorities to stop it."

In her pamphlet *The Great Scourge and How to End It* (1913), Christabel had written about a conspiracy of silence between men and doctors on the subject of sexually transmitted infections. The refusal to give women the knowledge, she maintained, was keeping them enslaved by debilitating illnesses:

"Innocent wives are infected by their husbands. They suffer torments; their health is ruined; their power to become mothers is destroyed, or else they become the mothers of diseased, crippled, blind, or insane children.

But they are not told the reason of all this. Their doctor and their husband keep them in ignorance, so that they cannot even protect themselves from future danger."

Christabel claimed in her pamphlet that 75–80 per cent of men were infected with sexually transmitted infections – some curable, some not – before marriage, and that "healthy women" were going into these marriages with no knowledge of the risks they would be incurring by sleeping with their husbands. She called for more openness and discussion of sex amongst men and women, for young women to be told about sex before marriage and for men to stop visiting prostitutes and to practise "chastity" before marriage, and fidelity within it. "In the opinion of the Suffragettes sex is too big and too sacred a thing to be treated lightly. Moreover, both the physical and spiritual consequences of a sex union are so important, so far-reaching, and so lasting, that intelligent and independent women will enter into such union only after deep consideration, and only when a great love and a great confidence are present."

There was talk in Parliament about how censorship could be enforced to stop Christabel's articles being published and about measures to suppress *The Suffragette*. Ramsay MacDonald, chairman of the Parliamentary Labour party, was so outraged by this attitude that he announced that if necessary he would "become manager of the National Labour Press, and publish *The Suffragette* and stand by the consequences".

It was not only in Parliament that the article was derided: many free-thinking suffragettes found it puritanical and counter to their philosophy of free love. The author Rebecca West was one of those who left the WSPU at around this time, feeling that Christabel was taking over the organization and transforming it into something no longer in sympathy with Rebecca's own views.

Chapter Eighteen

"Rebellion against tyrants is obedience to God."

Written on paper wrapped around stones thrown at
the MP David Lloyd George's car
by Emily Wilding Davison and friends

On a warm, sunny day in June 1913, people of all ages and classes
had gathered at Epsom racecourse. They were there to attend
one of the most eagerly anticipated events in the sporting calendar: the
Derby. Horse-racing may have been known as the "sport of kings" but
it was also the sport of the masses and, in those days before television
coverage, thousands of people had travelled from all over the country
to watch the day's racing. Amongst those in attendance were Queen
Mary and King George V, whose horse Anmer was being ridden in
the most anticipated race of the day by the talented jockey Herbert
"Diamond" Jones. Secreted amid the tens of thousands of spectators
was a contingent of suffragettes, many of whom had travelled together,
eager to raise the profile of their cause by protesting at important
and well-attended sporting events. Knowing that they would not be
allowed into the grounds if their suffragette status was recognized, they
kept the WSPU colours hidden away until they were safely inside the
racecourse.

Their number included a highly educated former school teacher, Emily Wilding Davison, who had given up her job some years previously to devote herself to the work of WSPU. She had become one of the cause's most prominent militant suffragists, setting fire to pillar boxes, smashing windows and being imprisoned for acts including hurling stones at a carriage in which the MP David Lloyd George was travelling, and planting a bomb. In January 1912, the newspapers had reported:

> *"Emily Wilding Davison, 36, tutor, was found guilty of placing matches and a packet smelling of kerosene in a Fleet-street letter-box ... and of attempting to place lighted matches in [a] Parliament-street letter-box.... The prosecution stated that Davison was a militant Suffragette, and had been previously convicted of offences arising out of the Suffragette movement. Otherwise her character was good.... Davison said there was not much chance of justice for women in a court composed of men."*

She was recorded as saying that she carried out the attacks in response to the fact that "three women had died as the result of injuries received during the raid on Parliament in November 1910".

Davison had also won the respect of her colleagues for successfully suing Strangeways prison for brutality. While on hunger strike, she had managed to resist force-feeding by barricading herself inside her cell. This so incensed the prison guards that a hosepipe was fed into her cell and freezing water pumped through it, which nearly drowned her. The reporting of this incident was one of the few instances of violence against suffrage prisoners that was taken seriously, and questions were asked in the House of Commons about why any prisoner was allowed to be subjected to such barbarism. When Davison sued Strangeways, the ruling found in her favour and she was awarded damages of 40 shillings. On the night of the 1911 census, when other suffragettes were protesting by keeping themselves hidden from the information gatherers, Emily Wilding Davison was discovered hiding in a broom cupboard at the House of Commons – her intention had been to stay there all night, so that she could declare on the census that her place of residence was the Houses of Parliament.[1]

On 4 June 1912, none of her WSPU colleagues had any inkling of what Davison was intending to do – although she had reportedly told her friend Mary Leigh, the day before, that she expected to make the newspapers on the evening of Derby Day. As the horses reached a bend in the course known as Tattenham Corner, Emily Wilding Davison stepped underneath the barrier and on to the course, where she waited for several horses to pass by before stepping out and grabbing the reigns of Anmer, the King's horse. It has been estimated that Anmer would have been travelling at a speed upwards of 35 miles per hour (over 55 kilometres per hour); whatever it was that Davison intended to do was thwarted by the fact that she was dragged underneath the horse's body, trampled by hooves and fatally injured.

The Daily Mirror, 5 June 1913

"The horse struck the woman with its chest, knocking her down among the flying hooves.… Blood rushed from her mouth and nose. Anmer turned a complete somersault and fell upon his jockey, who was seriously injured."

---

1. Many years later, Davison's "census sit-in" was commemorated by a plaque at the House of Commons. The wording on the plaque ends with a statement about Emily's death: "… to draw public attention to the injustice suffered by women. By such means was democracy won for the people of Britain." The plaque also displays part of the suffragette flag that Emily Wilding Davison wore at Epsom racecourse.

The Morning Post, 5 June 1913

"As the horses were making for Tattenham Corner a woman rushed out on the course in front of the King's horse Anmer, and put her hands above her head. The horse knocked her down and then turned a complete somersault on its jockey.... [The jockey] is suffering from concussion, and the woman, who had a Suffragist flag wrapped around her waist, is in a very serious condition in Epsom Cottage Hospital. The King made immediate enquiries regarding his jockey, who has no bones broken."

The Times, 5 June 1913

"The desperate act of a woman who rushed from the rails on to the course as the horses swept around Tattenham Corner, apparently from some mad notion that she could spoil the race, will impress the general public even more, perhaps, than the disqualification of the winner. She did not interfere with the race, but she nearly killed a jockey as well as herself, and she brought down a valuable horse.... That the horse was the King's was doubtless an accident: it would need almost miraculous skill or fortune to single out any particular animal as they passed.... Whether she intended to commit suicide, or was simply reckless, it is hard to surmise."

It seems most likely that what has long been claimed as a suicide was not intended to be so. Davison did not tell any of her friends or associates about her plan and much was made of the fact that a return train ticket was discovered in her pocket. She had bought a ticket to a suffragette social event after the Derby, suggesting she was not suicidal and intended to return home. The women standing close to her told police that they believed Davison was under the impression all the horses had gone past and was running out to make a statement or unfurl her banner. Her friends alleged that when she saw a new team of horses racing towards her she screamed and fainted – but the jockey saw her deliberately reach up and aim for the reins and it was that action which led to her being dragged under the horse. It seems Davison might naively have assumed she could stop or injure the King's horse, or simply that she intended to cause a sensation and stop the race. When she was being examined by doctors, suffragette flags were discovered tied around her waist; it seems likely she intended to unfurl these on the race track, or perhaps to attach a flag to the horse itself so that it would cross the finish line wearing the suffragette colours. It seems certain that Davison understood nothing about horses or the speeds they could attain. On the other side of the argument were those who reminded the newspapers about the times when Davison had seemed to risk her life while in prison, both by starving herself and by attempting to throw herself from a balcony – although her mental state while enduring a brutal imprisonment would have been very different from when outside the prison walls. The inquest on her death did not label her death as suicide.

Many years later Flora Drummond gave an interview to the Press Association in which she recalled: "I remember the day when poor Emily Wilding Davison came to my house and my mother gave her the purple, white and green flags. We did not know where she was going, but Emily went to the Derby and flung herself in front of the King's horse at Tattenham Corner and was killed."

Rebecca West wrote an article entitled "The Life of Emily Davison" in which she recalled a woman she had known personally through the WSPU.

"She was a wonderful talker. Her talk was an expression of that generosity which was her master passion.... She led a very ordinary life for a woman of her type and times. She was imprisoned eight times, she hunger-struck seven times; she was forcibly fed forty-nine times. That is the kind of life to which we dedicate our best and kindest and wittiest women; we take it for granted that they shall spend their kindness and their wits in ugly scuffles in dark cells."

In 1961, BBC Radio interviewed the dramatist St John Ervine about the fact that he happened to have been standing next to Davison seconds before her death. At the time he was working as a journalist and when his editor discovered Ervine had never been to the Derby he told him to go for the day. Ervine related that he had been rather bored and had started walking towards the railway station when he decided to stop and watch a race:

"As I was walking along towards Tattenham Corner there was a sudden hush, the most extraordinary silence I can remember and I realised that the horses had started ... I found myself standing beside a rather agitated woman, she was very pale and thin and she quite clearly was in a state of mental agitation, her name as I discovered the next day was Emily Davison. However I paid no particular heed to her and I looked up the course and saw these horses coming down ... like express trains and while they were running towards where I was standing, suddenly this woman went under the rails and as they came up she flung her hands up and it happened to be the King's horse.... And there was of course a rather horrid scene.... The amazing fact was that almost no one in the race ... saw it at all! I went on to the ... railway station,

went up to London and it was not until I got into London and into the office of the Pall Mall Gazette that I realised what a big story it was.... The whole thing was rather horrible, not something that anyone would want to see a second time."[2]

Contrary to common belief, Davison did not die on the turf. She was taken away, comatose, by stretcher and hospitalized in Epsom. Over the next few days, many newspapers proclaimed the government's intention of suing Davison should she recover, but the medical staff had few illusions about her ever recovering from such profound head injuries. Emily Wilding Davison died on 8 June 1913, four days after the Derby. She was 40 years old. Much was made of the fact that she had once told her friends and colleagues that, if the government did not recognize women's rights, the ultimate sacrifice would one day be necessary.

The WSPU took Davison's death as a battle cry. A book written in the year of her death, by fellow suffragette Gertrude Colmore, claimed that Davison had intended to martyr herself on the racecourse. (The book was published to capitalize on the tide of interest in the suffrage movement following Davison's death and cannot be seen as a faithful recording of Davison's own feelings.) When the WSPU published this biography of their fallen comrade, no mention was made of the tension that had existed for some time between Davison and the Pankhursts.

The jockey Herbert Jones suffered surprisingly light injuries: concussion from which he soon recovered and, amazingly given the reports of Anmer's "somersault", no broken bones. He received a telegram from Queen Alexandra, widow of the monarch so famed for his love of racing, King Edward VII. The telegram was reported to have expressed sorrow about the "sad accident caused through the abominable conduct of a brutal lunatic woman". Anmer survived and

---

2. Transcription of a BBC Radio interview with St John Ervine from 16 June 1961.

went on to race again, although he was notable for never winning a race. The horse believed to have won that year's Derby was Craganour – until the stewards disqualified him. The winner was then named as Aboyeur,[3] a rank outsider, leading to unsympathetic headlines in the newspapers such as "A Sensational Derby".

One of the reasons that Davison's act had such widespread repercussions was because it was captured on celluloid by a pioneering film-making enthusiast. Despite Davison's friends saying she believed the horses had all gone past, the footage shows quite clearly her climbing beneath the barrier, waiting as several horses thundered past, then decisively walking up to a specific horse and raising her hands.

The day of Davison's funeral was marked by the solemn splendour of a procession of mourning women. Many of the suffragettes had never met Davison, but they travelled to London to pay their respects to the women who had died for their cause. The WSPU had sent out a circular letter to other suffrage societies inviting them to attend the funeral:

June 11th, 1913
Dear Secretary,

The body of Miss Emily Wilding Davison will be taken across London on Saturday from Victoria to King's Cross.

Your Society will probably feel it an honour to take part in the procession, and in this way to testify to their reverence of this woman who has laid down her life for the Cause we all have at heart.

The procession will form up at 1 o'clock on the north side of Buckingham Palace Road opposite Victoria Station,

---

3. The National Horse Racing Museum records that Aboyeur was bought by a Russian owner after the Derby and that he "disappeared" during the Russian Revolution.

and will start at 2 o'clock punctually for St. George's, Hart Street, Bloomsbury, where a service will be held at 4 o'clock. Should your Society wish to attend, your place will be in <u>Section 1</u>.

The prevailing colour of the procession will be purple, and you are invited to veil your banner with that colour. Any wreaths brought should be carried by your representatives. White purple or black should be worn, and a black band on the left arm two inches in depth.
The admission to the church will be by ticket for which application must be made.

The route of the procession will be through Grosvenor Place, Piccadilly and Shaftesbury Avenue.

During the service the processionists for whom there is no accomodation [sic] in the church, will pass into Russell Square, and wait till the procession is over for the procession to move on to King's Cross, where the body will be entrained for Morpeth, Northumberland."[4]

The funeral took place on Saturday, 14 June. It was estimated that at least 6,000 women marched in memory of the dead suffragette and as many as 50,000 spectators were said to have watched them file through the streets of London to the accompaniment of brass bands. The service was held at St George's Church in Bloomsbury.[5] Then the coffin was transported to King's Cross station, where it began its journey,

---

4. This letter, sent to the London Society from the WSPU, can be seen in the collection at the Women's Library in London.

5. St George's Church, which was designed by Nicholas Hawksmoor, was at the heart of the socially conscious Christian movement in the 19th century, providing food and practical help for the poor and homeless.

together with a guard of suffragettes, to the Davison family's grave in Morpeth, Northumberland. On the memorial above Emily's name is the biblical inscription "Greater love hath no man than this, that a man lay down his life for his friends"; underneath her birth and death dates is inscribed "Deeds Not Words".

Rebecca West wrote of the funeral: "If, when we walked behind her bier on Saturday, we thought of ourselves as doing a dead comrade honour, we were wrong. We were making a march of penitence behind a victim we allowed the Government to do to death."

Chapter Nineteen

"To me there is something hateful, sinister, sickening in this heaping up of art treasures, this sentimentalising over the bodies of the beautiful, while the desecration and ruin of bodies of women ... are looked upon with indifference."[1]

Ethel Smyth, composer and suffragette, on why she took part
in attacking the Manchester Art Gallery in 1913

At the start of 1914, the suffrage world was rocked by yet another division in the WSPU – this time within the Pankhurst family. Emmeline and Christabel remained united, but Sylvia Pankhurst broke away from the organization and was frozen out by her mother and sister. For several years, Sylvia had been working with London's poorest East End communities and focusing on the class of women many suffragettes seemed to have forgotten about. She had formed the East London Federation of the WSPU, which had until now been working alongside the union as an affiliated branch. Now she decided – or was told – to separate her activities from those of the WSPU. This was big news all over

---

1. Quoted in "Suffragette Vandalism" by the Women's Library at londonmet.ac.uk

the English-speaking world. The *New York Times* reported on the rift:

> *"The split is all the more remarkable because it marks a division of opinion between the two sisters. While Christabel has been issuing instructions from Paris that the Women's Social and Political Union was to be kept independent of all political parties, the movement led by Sylvia has been showing Socialistic tendencies. The formation of a 'people's army', with the object of resisting alleged police brutality, was the latest of Sylvia's feats."*

For years, Sylvia had been frustrated by the pace of the suffrage fight. In her 1931 book *The Suffragette Movement* she would look back on the NUWSS and comment: "It was so staid, so willing to wait, so incorrigibly leisurely." Now she had fallen foul of WSPU. Like her mother and sister, Sylvia was an immensely strong woman and a born leader. The East London Federation of Suffragettes never became as influential as the organization run by her mother and sister, but Sylvia worked tirelessly at the project and at her social work among women in the poorest communities. She also founded her own journal, *Women's Dreadnought*. Many years later, following Sylvia's death in 1960 in Addis Ababa, Ethiopia (where she had been living for some years), the split was written about in her obituaries. The relationship between the Pankhurst women was something that, even many years after their shared campaign was won, still fascinated the public. Reuters wrote in their obituary:

> *"Estelle Sylvia was the most militant of the three Pankhursts.... She campaigned fervently for three causes: votes for women, unmarried mothers and Ethiopian independence. Miss Pankhurst was in the thick of nearly every deed of violence by the 'wild, wild women' who*

fought for female suffrage.... Miss Pankhurst was ready to go to any extreme to prove her case. She even joined the ranks of unmarried mothers for whom she was fighting by deliberately having a baby outside wedlock at the age of 45. To the end of her life, she kept the father's name secret – announcing only that he was 53 years old, a foreigner and 'an old and dear friend whom I have loved for years'.... Mrs Emmeline Pankhurst ... [was] adored by her daughter. But Sylvia's venture into free love caused a breach between them. During the suffrage campaign, Sylvia was sentenced to imprisonment 15 times and went on hunger strike 13 times."

On Wednesday, 11 March 1914, *The Times* reported on the latest outrage to have been committed by a suffragette. Mary Richardson, already a notorious member of the WSPU in the minds of the newspaper-reading public, had calmly walked into the National Gallery in London, taken from her bag a small hatchet and proceeded to slash at one of the most expensive paintings in the gallery, *The Toilet of Venus* (more commonly known as *The Rokeby Venus* as it had been bought for the gallery from Rokeby Hall in County Durham) by the Spanish artist Diego Velázquez. The picture, which was painted in 1647–51, had been bought in 1906 for a reputed £45,000. It depicts Venus, the goddess of love, lying naked and seen full-length with her back towards the viewer. A mirror is being held up in front of her by her son Cupid, so that she – and the viewer – can see her face. When it came to art, the Edwardians could be as hypocritical as their Victorian ancestors. Conventional public art galleries were still reluctant to display nude portraits, which were considered pornography, but if an artist painted a nude woman and gave her the name of a goddess, a gallery could get away with displaying even intensely erotic or pornographic paintings as art – the key thing was to ignore the fact that the artist had not painted the picture via divine intervention but had used a real, naked woman for the model.

Other visitors to the National Gallery stood transfixed with shock as Richardson slashed the painting multiple times. She had been inspired to attack the gallery out of fury at the treatment that Emmeline Pankhurst, once again back in prison, was enduring. Those who witnessed the attack and then watched Richardson wait calmly to be arrested related the words she had spoken: "You can get another picture, but you cannot get another life. They are killing Mrs Pankhurst." In her 1952 memoirs, Mary Richardson elaborated: "There was also another reason for choosing this picture. I didn't like the way men visitors to the gallery gaped at it all day."

The Times report began with the words:

> "*The famous Rokeby Velázquez, commonly known as the 'Venus with the Mirror', which was presented to the National Gallery in 1906, was mutilated yesterday morning by the prominent militant woman suffragist Mary Richardson. She attacked the picture with a small chopper with a long narrow blade, similar to the instruments used by butchers, and in a few seconds inflicted upon it severe if not irreparable damage. In consequence of the outrage the National Gallery will remain closed to the public until further notice.... Altogether the canvas has been slashed in six or seven places, the cuts extending from the top to the bottom of the picture.*"

The WSPU released an official statement from Mary Richardson which included the words: "I have tried to destroy the picture of the most beautiful woman in mythological history as a protest against the Government for destroying Mrs Pankhurst, who is the most beautiful character in modern history."

There was more public fury at the discovery that Mary Richardson should have been in prison for earlier offences, but had been released under the Cat and Mouse Act and had not been rearrested, thereby leaving her free to slash the painting. Henry Duveen, one of the most prominent art dealers in London, was interviewed about the attack on the painting while he was sailing to England on board the *Lusitania*:[2]

> *"The painting can be repaired, but it will reduce its value to the British nation considerably. Since last Summer the authorities in charge of the National Gallery had a number of the most valuable paintings packed away in anticipation of some wilful mischief of this kind. I expect that the result of this ... will be that the gallery will either be closed, or that the most valuable pictures will be put aside and kept under guard."*

All over the country, tourist attractions began closing their doors to the public. Many only allowed men to enter – and then only men of the upper classes, who were deemed less likely to be "in league" with the militant suffragists. The House of Commons closed the doors of its Ladies' Gallery to anyone except those vouched for personally by an MP. A surviving letter (now in the Women's Library in London) from the MP Viscount Greenwood to an acquaintance, Alfred Miles, who had asked him to vouch for one of his friends, illustrates the general caution:

> *"I am very sorry I cannot send an Order for the lady friend to whom you refer. I have no doubt she is*

---

2. The ill-fated *Lusitania*, a passenger ship, was torpedoed by a German U-boat in May 1915. More than a thousand people died as the ship sank.

everything you say and I should personally like to oblige her, but owing to the unreasonable outbreaks of extreme women I have declined sending Orders for the Ladies Gallery to anyone except my immediate family circle."
(11 March 1914)

When the newspapers reported that Mary Richardson was gravely ill[3] through refusal to eat and force-feeding, they expected their readers to have little compassion. She had been on hunger strike since her arrest and many times previously, having been arrested nine times for offences including arson and bombing. And indeed, just a couple of weeks after Richardson's imprisonment, press accounts that she was being released because she needed an appendectomy brought an outcry. Several newspapers reported reactions from the public, such as the now-famous headline "Let Them Starve". [4] Nonetheless, "Slasher Mary", as the newspapers dubbed her, went on to write her memoirs in the 1950s, in which she commented that she visited the National Gallery from time to time and looked proudly at the still-visible marks of her hatchet-work.

Sylvia Pankhurst later chronicled the suffragette activities of 1914, which was a year of ferocious militancy on an unprecedented scale: "One hundred and forty-one acts of destruction were chronicled in the Press during the first seven months of 1914," she related. The

---

3. Mary Richardson survived prison and lived to the age of 81. After joining the Labour party after the war, she stood for Parliament several times, but was never elected – some years later she was briefly a supporter of the Fascist leader Oswald Mosley. She died in 1961, at her home in Hastings, Sussex, where her body was discovered in "a gas-filled room", leading to speculation as to whether it had been an accident or suicide.

4. In the collection of the Museum of London is a newspaper billboard from the London *Evening Standard*, dated Tuesday, 9 June (year not given but believed to be 1914), proclaiming "'Let Them Starve' Views of Public Men".

most serious acts included Helen Crawford being arrested after a bomb exploded in the Botanic Gardens in Glasgow and Annie Ball – who had been released temporarily from prison under the Cat and Mouse Act – placing a bomb under a pew at the Church of St John the Evangelist in Westminster: the bomb did not explode, but she told the court she had intended to "blow up the church". The anti-suffragists capitalized on the public's disgust for militant suffragism and some members of the public continued to fight back. On 12 June 1914, Miss Winterbourne, a suffrage campaigner who lived and worked in Balham, hosted an evening suffrage meeting in her house. After the meeting, the house was attacked by a furious mob.

The NUWSS tried desperately to remind people that there was an enormous difference between suffragists and suffragettes. They intended to keep their campaign strong, but overtly non-violent. On 21 May 1914, Lady Willoughby-Broke, a suffragist and the wife of a Conservative MP, wrote to her friend Mrs Cavendish Bentinck about her own form of protest. The editor of *The Times* kept requesting details of Lord and Lady Willoughby-Broke's social engagements but, as he refused to publish any details about the political work she and her husband ("Grev") were involved in, she refused to tell him any of the details he wanted. She wrote to Mrs Cavendish Bentinck:

"I just must tell you how enormously I have enjoyed your going and wiping the floor with 'The Times' Editor. Several times they have sent me the ridiculous request that my Secretary should keep them posted as to our doings. I replied indignantly some 18 months ago, that as they did not consider either my speeches or work, or Grev's, worth reporting, when connected with important National affairs, such as Women's Suffrage, National Service, etc., I did not think that it could possibly be of any interest to the general public to report the fact that we had lunched or dined at any particular place. In spite of this, they have several times repeated their

request, which I now put in the waste-paper basket. You will remember how Grev. trounced them in the House of Lords the other day for not properly reporting the Bishop of London's admirable Suffrage speech. This hit them on the raw, and they had a very peevish protest in their paper the next day. They rang me up on the telephone on Sunday in connection with my reply to Mrs. [Humphry] Ward. Grev gave them beans down the telephone and told them if they did not put it on the front page he should expose them in the Press, so altogether they are having a bad time.... Mrs Humphry Ward's second letter yesterday was feeble. She does not attempt to refute mine and, luckily, I possess an extremely valuable letter of hers on the subject of her ridiculous Local Government Advancement Society, in which she herself uses the words 'Anti-Suffrage Candidates selected by an Anti-Suffrage Committee'."[5]

In May 1914, the WSPU presented a petition to King George V. It protested against the force-feeding of hunger strikers, asked for "equal treatment for the militant Ulster men and militant suffragists" and demanded votes for women. Emmeline Pankhurst carried the petition to the gates of Buckingham Palace, cheered on by a large crowd of supporters; she was one of over 60 women arrested that day. The photograph of this frail-looking but furious little woman being carried by a burly policeman away from what was recognizably the royal palace made newspapers all over the world. This was to be the last important WSPU action for a while. On 4 August 1914, Britain went to war with Germany.

---

5. This letter can be seen in the collection at the Women's Library in London.

On 5 August 1914, *The Guardian* informed its readers:

> *"Great Britain declared war on Germany at 11 o'clock last night. The Cabinet yesterday delivered an ultimatum to Germany. Announcing the fact to the House of Commons, the Prime Minister said: 'We have repeated the request made last week to the German Government that they should give us the same assurance in regard to Belgian neutrality that was given to us and Belgium by France last week. We have asked that it should be given before midnight.*
>
> *'Last evening a reply was received from Germany. This being unsatisfactory the King held at once a Council which had been called for midnight. The declaration of war was then signed.'"*

The WSPU announced an immediate cessation of all militant activities and Emmeline Pankhurst underwent what appeared to many to be an immediate conversion from rebel to patriot, working closely with the government. On the same day that war was declared, 4 August 1914, suffragists from many of the different societies united with other pacifists for a peace meeting that had already been arranged in London. The speakers, several from overseas, condemned what they saw as the "unstoppable" force of war and what would happen to the women and children of Europe – none of whom had been given any say in what they thought about the conflict. A Swiss member of the International Women's Suffrage Alliance, Mme Thoumaian, voiced the thoughts of many of the women present in her speech: "Everyone is speaking of war as if it were a dispensation from the Almighty, something like measles, that we cannot avoid, and so must accept with patience."

Chapter Twenty

"I have all my life felt very strongly the injustice &
stupidity of keeping women out of any kind of work,
for which they happened to be indubitably fit, and of
making any distinction between them & men, once
they were admitted. The recommendation of the Royal
Commission is very moderate. Personally I should be
prepared to go further, & without encouraging women
to go in for what has always been regarded as men's
work, to recognise that there are a large number of
women who have a natural inclination & aptitude for
such work, & should be allowed to do it on terms of
absolute equality."

Millicent Garrett Fawcett in a letter to Lord Milner,
19 July 1915[1]

War introduced a whole new level of complexity for the women's
movement – although ultimately it was to provide a crucial
catalyst for much-striven-for change. In 1914, all over the country,

---

1. This letter can be seen in the collection at the Women's Library in London.

women were discussing what kind of war work they should sign up for and how they could continue to fight for female suffrage without appearing unpatriotic by rocking the national boat. For those with pacifist beliefs, the balancing act was even more delicate. During the war, the fight for women's suffrage was primarily kept going by the NUWSS, whose followers continued to campaign for the vote at the same time as carrying out war work.

Despite the fact that all the suffrage societies encouraged their members to take an active part in war work of some sort, the very mention of the words "women's suffrage" was inflammatory in the country at large, perceived as something that should be forgotten while the nation was at war. When the NUWSS was planning an outdoor meeting, Mrs Ford wrote to Millicent Garrett Fawcett about her fears that she was putting herself in danger by speaking at such an event: "Dearest Millie, We are thinking so anxiously about you today – about the Park meeting. Christabel wouldn't face, doesn't face, these angry crowds. I wish I could be there too – in my active service dress, which I've now got...."[2]

Some women, as suffragists and pacifists, debated whether, in the circumstances, tax resistance was a good idea. Philippa Strachey sent a letter to an NUWSS member, Mrs Cliff, who had written asking whether she would still be keeping the "law-abiding" agreement for suffragists during the war if she refused to pay tax:

"Dear Mrs Cliff,

I have consulted the Executive Committee with regard to your letter of the 6th Instant, and they consider that the meaning of the word "law-abiding" in regard to tax resistance must be left to each member to interpret individually as the matter appeals to his or her under-standing.

---

2. This letter can be seen in the collection at the Women's Library in London.

You are no doubt aware that the N.U.W.S.S. discussed the policy of tax resistance at a National Council Meeting a year or two ago and decided not to adopt it."

On 5 August 1914, Lord Robert Cecil wrote an angry letter to his friend Millicent Garrett Fawcett. Until this time he had been a firm ally, but the fact that the NUWSS had joined in the Peace Meeting of the day before had infuriated him:

"Action of that kind will undoubtedly make it very difficult for the friends of Women's Suffrage in both the Unionist and Ministerial parties. Even to me the action seems so unreasonable under the circumstances as to shake my belief in the fitness of women to deal with great Imperial questions & I can only console myself by the belief that in this matter the National Union do not represent the opinions of their fellow country women."[3]

Interestingly, Mrs Pankhurst seemed to abandon the fight for votes for women during the war, devoting her energies instead into helping the government with recruitment. Both she and Christabel found themselves respecting and working with pro-war politicians whose anti-suffrage stances they had both despised pre-1914. In 1915, Emmeline Pankhurst had a meeting with David Lloyd George, the Chancellor of the Exchequer, at which it was agreed that a payment of £4,000 would be made by the Treasury to the WSPU – in return for which its leaders would galvanize women to encourage men to join up. In the Call to Women march of July 1915, tens of thousands of women

---

3. This letter can be seen in the collection at the Women's Library in London.

marched through London wearing red, white and blue – and noticeably without encountering any confrontations with the police. In the same year, as a display of patriotism, Christabel changed the name of her *The Suffragette* newspaper to *Britannia*. She also encouraged her followers no longer to throw stones, but instead to hand out white feathers, as a symbol of cowardice, to any man not in uniform or not obviously injured. The war caused the rift between Sylvia and her mother and sister to widen even further, as Sylvia was utterly opposed to the war and to the actions of both Emmeline and Christabel.

Sylvia Pankhurst was active, however, as part of a campaign to protest against the army imposing unfair legislation on soldiers' wives. She spoke to the government about the injustice of having a law that sought to control women's lives without introducing any such restrictions upon men (the laws included a ban on women drinking alcohol in public). Lord Kitchener gave his consent to Sylvia and the other delegates being admitted into the War Office to voice their concerns. Several affiliated branches of the NUWSS set up Women's Patriotic Clubs, to help the relatives of soldiers and sailors. In January 1915, the *Western Daily Press* reported:

> *"Over 1,300 voluntary workers have registered their names at the Bureau for Voluntary Workers opened at the outbreak of the war by the London Society for Women Suffrage under their Women's Service scheme. Of these all but a few have been drafted to service with one of the many organisations employed in social work, while 320 organisations and individuals have been supplied with much needed helpers."*

Volunteer activities were legion. Suffragists from all over the country organized ambulance corps and sent out volunteer medical crews to help take care of the wounded soldiers in Europe. Dr Louisa Garrett Anderson and Dr Flora Murray set up the Women's Hospital

Corps. Other groups included the Women's Volunteer Reserve, the Women's Sick and Wounded Convoy Corps, the Women's Institute (which was founded to help women in rural communities understand about food production) and the Women's Defence Relief Corps. Emmeline Pethick-Lawrence and others set up the Women's Emergency League – whilst also campaigning for peace and an end to all wars – and Lady Bertha Dawkins set up classes to teach women welding and other essential jobs previously all filled by men and much needed in war time.

Under the headline "What Women Can Do", the *Manchester Courier* reported:

> *"A remarkable variety of useful work has been performed by the Women's Emergency Corps.... They have borrowed theatres, offices, houses, established scores of work-homes for women, the takings from which amount to something between £50 and £60 a week. They have dressed hundreds of needy people, established a band of women interpreters, and are teaching languages to 15,000 recruits in London, as well as having classes in every big camp in the country. By means of forming a training centre for girls … the Emergency Corps has enabled 400 girls to take their nursing certificates. Then there are the thousands of handy-women, 250 lady motorists who can drive and do all their own repairs, 30 equally experienced motor cyclists and 480 horsewomen, who can groom horses and do stable work. A volunteer reserve trained in telegraphy, who can be relied upon in an emergency to guard bridges, should be added to the list. By collecting London's waste food from the markets they are feeding something like 1,500 people a day, and at one place they provide six hot dinners at a penny each. The corps also runs a housecraft scheme, pays £30 a week to knitters, has fitted out the Canadian*

Contingency Hospital, and handed over a yacht to the Admiralty. 'Mere man' will be surprised to learn that all this work has been done by an organisation which started with a capital of £10."

The Women's Emergency Corps had been the idea of WSPU member Evelina Haverfield, who became famous both for the khaki uniform she wore and her inexhaustible energy, which even took her to Serbia to work with the remarkable Dr Elsie Maud Inglis and her recruits for the Scottish Women's Hospitals. The latter was partly funded by the NUWSS, after Dr Inglis's application to the War Office was refused – reportedly the official told her to "go home and sit still – no petticoats here". This conversation took place six decades after Florence Nightingale had persuaded the War Office to allow her to take her nurses out to work in the Crimea; the government seemed to have gone back over half a century.

Many suffragists were also pacifists and as such empathized with the plight of those men imprisoned as conscientious objectors. Mary Barbour founded the Women's Peace Crusade, an anti-war group concerned about the effect of war on families, homes and jobs. One of the ways in which the NUWSS was able to help was to provide a woman to carry on the man's job while he was in prison, with the understanding the job would be his again once he was released. The Labour MP Walter Henry Ayles was one of those imprisoned for refusing to fight. His letter of February 1917, thanking Millicent Garrett Fawcett for her help, has survived:

"Dear Madam,

It has been reported to me since my release from Wandsworth Prison that the NUWSS council have endorsed the generous action of the Executive, permitting Mrs Townley to do my work while I am away from

Bristol. May I say how deeply I appreciate their action & also that of yourself. I can understand how keenly you must feel on the great war question – as keenly as I feel in the opposite direction. That only emphasises the breadth and generosity of the spirit behind your action. To me it is full of profound import for the success of the womens' [sic] movement & I trust that the time is not far distant when I shall be able once again to do my little towards its complete achievement.

Believe me yours faithfully, Walter H. Ayles"[4]

At the start of the conflict, the War Office had been reluctant to allow women to take on "men's" jobs, partly because they were convinced, with astonishing naivety, that the war would come to an end far more quickly than it did. By the end of the war, nonetheless, it was estimated that two million more women had joined the British workforce – although they were consistently paid far lower wages than their male counterparts for exactly the same jobs.

While Millicent Garrett Fawcett continued to campaign for women's suffrage, a campaign she believed should be boosted by the invaluable work women were performing all over the country and overseas, Prime Minister Asquith continued to oppose it at every turn. On 7 May 1916, he sent her the following letter in response to her request that women be granted the vote now they had proved themselves by their war work:

---

4. This letter can be seen in the collection at the Women's Library in London. In the 1920s, Walter Henry Ayles published books including *What a Socialist Town Council Would Do* and *Why I Worked for Peace During the Great War*. In the 1930s, he was appointed Secretary of the No More War Movement.

"... I need not assure you how deeply my colleagues and I recognise and appreciate the magnificent contribution which the women of the United Kingdom have made to the maintenance of our country's cause.

No such legislation as you refer to is at present in contemplation, but if, and when, it should become necessary to undertake it, you may be certain that the considerations set out in your letter will be fully and impartially weighed, without any bejudgment from the controversies of the past."[5]

Within a few months, however, everything had changed for Asquith. On 7 December 1916, following furious attacks on his method of government – both in the war and in Ireland – the beleaguered Asquith resigned. He was replaced as Prime Minister by the former Chancellor of the Exchequer, David Lloyd George, who had also been Minister of Munitions and Secretary of State for War since the conflict had begun. Lloyd George had grown increasingly critical of Asquith's handling of the war, and as a result many accused him of plotting against Asquith.[6] For the suffrage campaigners, the resignation of Herbert Henry Asquith could not have come too soon.

Following the appointment of the new Prime Minister, interesting letters were sent by and to Lord Northcliffe, the media baron, in which he appears to be agitating for suffrage campaigns to start up again. The letters form part of the collection at the Women's Library in London.

---

5. This letter can be seen in the collection at the Women's Library in London.

6. Within a few years, the Liberal party would be divided, between those who supported Lloyd George and those who supported Asquith. This would lead to a Conservative win in the 1922 General Election and to the Labour party gaining a large number of new voters.

On 22 December 1916, Lord Northcliffe wrote to Lady Betty Balfour:

"**Dear Lady Betty,**

There is absolutely no movement for Women's Suffrage anywhere. I have made enquiries of a great many women on the subject, but they do not take any interest in it. I cannot explain the psychology, but it is the fact. Try and get up a public meeting on the subject, and I will support it, and you will soon find out whether I am right or wrong.

Yours sincerely, Northcliffe"

The content of this letter was soon reported to Millicent Garrett Fawcett, who was incensed by his attitude and railed that men were entirely unreasonable in expecting active suffrage agitation (over and above correspondence with politicians) at a time of war. On Christmas Day 1916, Lord Northcliffe wrote again to Lady Betty:

"**Dear Lady Betty,**

I have written to Mrs Fawcett to defend my sex against her unjust accusation that we men are unreasonable. Personally I think myself one of the most reasonable of men.

Seriously, I think that some kind of manifestation is necessary.

I am going to read Mrs Fawcett's letter at the Prime Minister to-morrow.

Yours sincerely, Northcliffe"

His letter to Millicent Garrett Fawcett read:

"Dear Mrs Fawcett,

I hope you will allow me to waive ceremony and defend my "unreasonable" sex against your attack, which has reached me through Lady Betty.

I do not suggest window-breaking, but I do think that some great meeting or united deputation is necessary.

Public psychology is such that people can only think of one thing at a time. They are now thinking only of the war. And it is quite possible that legislation will arrive unnoticed that may be detrimental to the interests not only of women, but to many other sections of the community. Lady Betty has asked me to speak to the Prime Minister and I will do so to-morrow.

Yours sincerely, Northcliffe"

On 26 December, Millicent Garrett Fawcett wrote a reply to his letter:

"Dear Lord Northcliffe

Thank you for writing to me and giving me your advice. I am to meet the other officers of the Nat Union of W.S. Societies on Friday morning and will then more carefully consider your letter.

I believe that as a consequence of the experiences of the last 29 months, women's suffrage has attained quite a new and a far stronger position that ever before, and that this is due not only to good work done by women but to the good spirit in which it has been done, the spirit or whole-hearted love of our country and reverence for its aims in this war.... We must beware of acting in any way calculated to weaken this impression; and from this point of view I incline to the big deputation rather than a public meeting."

Lord Northcliffe spoke to the Prime Minister on the evening of 26 December and wrote identical letters to both Lady Betty Balfour and Millicent Garrett Fawcett the following morning:

"I talked for some time last night with the Prime Minister who is very keen on the subject and practical, too.

I make the suggestion to you ... that you get up a large and representative Deputation. That will give the newspapers the opportunity of dealing with the matter.

I shall speak to the Editor of the Times on the question to-day. I believe he is entirely favourable."

He also wrote an undated note to Millicent Garrett Fawcett giving her permission to use his name "in connection with any other meetings you may have".

At last, the women's movement could start to feel hopeful. In June 1917, the Hon. Arthur Stanley MP wrote to Pippa Strachey saying he would be pleased to see her "and friends" at 1 Kensington Palace Gardens on the following Friday. On 19 June, the House of Commons voted to accept the women's suffrage clause in the Representation of the

People Bill's: the move was passed by 385 in favour versus 55 against. The beginning of the final stage had begun and the mood within the women's movement was buoyant.

On 19 December 1917, the suffrage campaigner Mrs H. M. Swanwick sent a fond letter to Millicent Garrett Fawcett:

> *"I want at this time to be allowed to express once again the affectionate regard which I must always have for you and your work. The women's movement in England is what it is because you have lived & Englishwomen are going to be among the world's pioneers. Many things dear to us go under in war-time but the spirit of the women's movement will keep alive, I believe, & help to make a settlement in which all these things & more may emerge."*

The letter was sent at a poignant time when Millicent was in need of love and support: her sister Elizabeth Garrett Anderson had died on 17 December, at the age of 81.

Chapter Twenty One

"Many writers, novelists, poets and dramatists have represented the uttermost tragedy of human life as due to the incomprehensible contrariness of the feminine nature. The kindly ones smile, perhaps a little patronizingly, and tell us that women are more instinctive, more child-like, less reasonable than men. The bitter ones sneer or reproach or laugh at this 'contrariness' in women they do not understand, and which, baffling their intellect, appears to them to be irrational folly."

Marie Stopes from *Married Love*, 1918

On 26 January 1918, David Lloyd George sent a letter to Millicent Garrett Fawcett:

"My wife has forwarded to me from the country the very kind letter which you addressed to her. I deeply appreciate your warm references to the part it has been my privilege to take in forwarding the cause of Woman Suffrage. I shall always be proud to think that a Government of which I am the head undertook the responsibility of promoting and

carrying through a measure for redeeming pledges which I personally gave to thousands of women at a meeting over which you presided at the Albert Hall. I meant it then. I thank you because you were convinced of my good faith at the time."[1]

After decades of battles, the long fight for female suffrage was won – at least in part.

The Representation of the People Act had long been due for an overhaul and, with the war looking as though it might, finally, be coming to an end, the government was faced with a burning issue: unless the old act was overhauled, when the millions of soldiers began to return home, having risked their lives and lost so many of their comrades, many would be arriving back to a country in which they had no entitlement to vote. The act needed to be rewritten so that property qualifications for men were abolished.

On 6 February 1918, the new Representation of the People Act became law. It entitled all men aged over 21 – except those in prison – to vote. In addition, women over 30 who met the minimum property qualifications were also entitled to vote. Before the new act, 7.7 million men had been entitled to vote in Britain; after the Representation of the People Act 1918, that number had swelled to a voting population of 21.4 million men and women.[2] Even before the war, there had been more women than men in the British Isles. Following the deaths of around one million British men in the so-called Great War, that percentage had increased dramatically. The act included the clause:

---

1. This letter can be seen in the collection at the Women's Library in London.

2. Figures from www.parliament.uk

"4.(1) A woman shall be entitled to be registered as a parliamentary elector for a constituency (other than a university constituency) if she –

(a) has attained the age of thirty years; and

(b) is not subject to any legal incapacity; and

(c) is entitled to be registered as a local government elector in respect of the occupation in that constituency of land and premises (not being a dwelling-house) of a yearly value of not less than five pounds or of a dwelling-house, or is the wife of a husband entitled to be so registered."

On 7 February 1918, Ida Beatrice O'Malley, who worked for *The Common Cause*, wrote an excited letter to Lady Strachey:

"Isn't it glorious! It seems impossible to believe that Women's Suffrage is now a law of the land, but we shall believe it when we are walking into the Polling Station in our Ward of the Borough of Hampstead. I hope we shall have someone better to vote for than Mr Fletcher.

We are printing a special celebration number of the 'Common Cause' at the time of the Council meeting, and I am collecting messages for it from suffragists, statesmen and others. Will you be so very kind as to let me have a message from you to print with those from Mrs Fawcett, Miss Emily Davies and others?

You must be very pleased to think that the name of Strachey has been so closely associated with <u>every</u> stage of this great struggle. We all feel very proud of our Parliamentary Secretary!

With love and congratulations,
Yours affectionately,
I. B. O'Malley"[3]

On the same day, Miss Catherine E. Marshall wrote a warm letter to Millicent Garrett Fawcett:

"Dear Mrs Fawcett,

I suspect one of the first thoughts in the minds of all Suffragists today – at any rate of all members of the National Union – is one of thankfulness that the enfranchisement of women has come whilst you are still with us to see this fruition of your life-long work & leadership. And you will see more fruits than the actual obtaining of the vote. Though the struggle to remove the barrier has seemed long & wasteful of energies that we were all longing to use for constructive work, one can see how, looking backward, that the process of this struggle in itself gave us experience – even those of us who only came into it during the last decade – which ought to prove almost as valuable as the actual gain of the vote itself. It taught us, as perhaps nothing else could have taught us, the real value of liberty & the disastrous results of its

---

3. This letter can be seen in the collection at the Women's Library in London.

denial. It ought to have given us a deep insight into, &
sympathy with, the sufferings of all who are oppressed &
denied justice & an understanding of the difficulties of
all minorities seeking to alter their status quo.

You personally have taught us, by your wonderful example,
the invincible might of <u>patience</u> – not the patience that
is content to let wrong continue, but the patience that is
founded on indomitable faith that right <u>must</u> triumph.
You have taught us how to keep that faith undimmed
through disappointments and betrayals, & above all how
to keep our hearts free from bitterness."[4]

Not all suffrage campaigners were quite so thrilled, however. Many of the "old guard", including Dora Montefiore and Sylvia Pankhurst, were angry at the suffrage leaders for agreeing to accept what they considered such elitist terms. What they had striven for was votes for *all*, and that had most certainly not been achieved. Millicent Garrett Fawcett and her followers were convinced, however, that this was just the beginning. Now that a large percentage of the country's women had been given the vote, they would be able to use those votes to help ensure that – someday soon – all women, no matter what their social class or economic situation might be, would be enfranchised to the same level as men.

The WSPU, meanwhile, sent a message to its supporters claiming the victory entirely for itself and making no mention of the other suffrage societies; as far as the WSPU was concerned, it was their militant methods that had secured women the vote:

---

4. This letter can be seen in the collection at the Women's Library in London.

"The W.S.P.U by its pre-war crusade for the Vote, followed by its patriotic stand and national service during the War, has won the greatest political victory on record.

Under its new name of 'The Women's Party', the W.S.P.U. has now even greater work to do, for it has to ensure that the Women's vote shall be of the utmost possible service in protecting the industrial and other interests of women, and in securing the progress and safety of the nation as a whole.

Indeed we need not remind you that everything depends on how the vote is used, now that it has been won."

On 25 February 1918, a message went out from the Prime Minister to "the Women Electors of Great Britain and Ireland":

"I am delighted to send a message to the new women electors just enfranchised by the Reform Act. I have no doubt that they will rise to their new responsibilities in political life as successfully as they have risen to their responsibilities in the war. People sometimes think that voting is a thing that anybody can do without much difficulty; on the contrary, it is one of the most fateful acts in the citizen's life. On the way he or she casts the vote at times of election, directly depends the character and policy of the national government. If we are to have good government in this country, it will be because the voters have studied and thought about political problems and have thereby equipped themselves with the knowledge and understanding necessary to ensure that sound principles are predominant in the conduct of their national affairs.

There are many subjects upon which it is essential that the opinions of women should be brought directly to bear. I need only mention education, public health, housing, and the manifold problems connected with the welfare of infants and children, and I trust that women will make their influence felt on these matters without delay.

I need hardly say how much I welcome the passage of the Reform Act. I believe that responsible women voters can bring into public life a point of view and a spirit which will be of incalculable value to the progress of democracy in these islands."

On 13 March 1918, the suffrage societies joined together to hold a victory party at the Queen's Hall in London. A new hymn had been chosen as their suffrage song. During the war, musician Sir Hubert Parry had composed music to accompany words written by the Romantic artist and poet William Blake. The song, known by its new title "Jerusalem", became the women's song. (After 1928, it became the anthem for the Women's Institute.)

Another ground-breaking development for women in 1918 was the publication of the book *Married Love*[5] by scientist and birth-control campaigner Marie Stopes, described in Dr William J. Robinson's introduction to the book as a "sexologist". The sex manual, which advocated contraception and choices about family planning, was dedicated to "young husbands and all those who are betrothed in love". Despite being condemned by the church, the state and even a large number of doctors, the book was an immediate success. Stopes, who described her book's object as "to increase the joys of marriage, and to show how much sorrow may be avoided", was overwhelmed by the number of letters she received asking for more advice. In his

---

5. The book was banned in America until 1931.

introduction Dr Robinson commented: "It would be too soon to expect any one work to succeed in converting every home from the hell that it often is into the paradise that it should be; but … if it saves a few homes from disruption, it will be decidedly worth while, and its author will be called blessed – and will deserve to be."

Another important legal change in 1918 was the passing of the Parliamentary Qualification of Women Act, which enabled women to stand as MPs. The first general election at which women in Britain were entitled to vote took place on 14 December 1918. Countess Constance de Markiewicz became the first woman to be elected to Westminster, representing Sinn Fein – she did not, however, take her seat. Christabel Pankhurst also stood, as the Women's Party Candidate for the constituency of Smethwick; she was not elected. Thus the first woman to become a Member of Parliament was Lady Nancy Astor, in November 1919. She proclaimed in her pre-election literature:

> "I intend to work for the Peace, Progress and Prosperity of the Country. I shall, at the same time, have due regard to National Efficiency and Economy which women above all understand. During the war I worked for the soldiers and sailors, and their wives and children, as well as all the others who were serving at home and abroad. I now ask them to work for me in order that I may work for them in Parliament."

In a letter to Miss Rosenfeld, dated 8 December 1919, she commented that she was hoping for the support and co-operation of "all my friends and even my enemies".

Life for women was changing at a tremendous pace. For some, the changes were almost dizzying. In November 1920, the artist Kate Perugini, daughter of Charles Dickens, was asked to give a speech about the women in her father's novels. After realizing that ill health would prevent her from attending the event (she had just celebrated her 81st birthday), she decided to write a speech to be read out in her absence. It was entitled "On Women Old and New" and in it she wrote of the admiration she felt for those "daring" Victorian women who had broken the rules, citing Harriet Martineau and Florence Nightingale among them. She ruminated on the differences between the majority of women in Victorian Britain and those she called the "new splendid race of women" who willingly took the places of men called up to fight and did such an admirable job of keeping the country going in their absence – despite having been denied such opportunities before. Although Mrs Perugini deplored the militant methods used by the suffragettes, she applauded the fact that women had finally been allotted their "rightful place by man's side" and she called upon men not to complain or to reminisce over the meeker, more compliant women of the past (such as the unrealistic, idealized heroines in her father's novels), but to realize and appreciate that the 1920s woman was "a new and better edition" of those women the men had left behind when they went away to war. Her speech, which was published in the Dickens Fellowship's magazine *The Dickensian*, included the words: "Not a few of the Victorian ladies were timid and took rather roundabout ways in getting their ends, whereas, the new women go direct to the point and are unafraid. But you can never tell – perhaps they may be trembling in their very decorative shoes all the time, in spite of their commanding looks and martial stride."

In 1921, two years after Lady Astor had been elected to Parliament, another general election was expected within the next 12 months. The suffrage campaigners were as busy as they had been in the past, attempting to gain support for potential candidates. Pippa Strachey wrote to Millicent Garrett Fawcett about the reactions NUWSS members had experienced when questioning people as to what they thought of having a woman MP in their constituency:

> *"Our object is to visit as many village women as we can & we find it a constant surprise, we meet with so much intelligence and general information. One labourer's*

wife said that what she liked about Lady Astor was that she put Sir Frederick Banbury in his place! ... Lady Astor seems to be a general favourite. Two separate men have told me that they greatly disliked her getting in & completely disapproved of her at first, but now think she is the best member in the House. I suppose it must be her spirit that they admire. We were greatly pleased with an agricultural labourer who recognised our colours and said that he wished we had got Mrs Fawcett in Parliament, but added that you were so wise you no doubt had a good reason for not being.... In the villages there seems very little objection either among men or women to the idea of a woman M.P. One man calmly observed, 'I should be glad to see fifty more get in', & in general it seems to be accepted quite naturally."
(11 September 1921, Women's Library)

With women finally in the House of Commons and at the polling booths, legislation started to change. In 1920, the Sex Discrimination Removal Act allowed women access to the legal profession and to become accountants. In 1922, the Law of Property Act was passed, which gave men and women equal rights to inherit one another's property, and to inherit the property of any children who died intestate. (Four years later women would be granted the legal right to hold and to dispose of property on the same terms as men.) In 1923, an amended Matrimonial Causes Act finally made the grounds for divorce the same for men and women. Caroline Norton, who had died in 1877, would have been very proud. At the end of that year, Lady Astor had written to the suffragist Mrs Acres about the recent legislative changes, commenting, "We ought to do much better now, with eight women in the House."

In 1921, a new type of equality had been mooted: a new law was proposed that would make lesbian acts a criminal offence of "gross indecency", thereby affording women the same discrimination as that meted out to "practising" homosexual men. The House of Lords rejected the proposal – one of their reasons for doing so was that it was felt that simply passing such a bill would make people talk about lesbianism, which would mean a much larger percentage of the population would become aware of it and therefore it might be encouraged amongst women who might otherwise remain in ignorance of its very existence.

Sex was firmly on the political agenda. On 17 March 1921, Marie Stopes opened the very first birth-control clinic in Britain. The idea that people should be entitled to limit the size of their families was an issue that had been raging for decades – a very young and idealistic John Stuart Mill had been arrested and briefly imprisoned in the 1820s for distributing information about birth control to married working people – but it was something that had seldom made it into the newspapers, until now. Britain's first birth-control clinic was on Marlborough Road in Holloway, North London. It provided a free contraceptive and advice service – but only to married women.[6] Stopes had spawned a new industry, and by 1930 five family-planning charities had been set up and clinics had been opened all over the country. All were run under the same principle: "children by choice, not chance". The poster for Stopes's clinic proclaimed, "The Free Clinic is under the patronage of a distinguished Committee, staffed with qualified Lady Doctors and Certified Midwives," and also recommended women to read the *Birth Control News* – "ask for it at the Railway Bookstalls" – at a price of sixpence. Stopes's controversial *Married Love* had been a publishing sensation, despite great opposition. In 1922, she published *Wise Parenthood, the Treatise on Birth Control for Married People*. Suddenly, women were being given one of the most important choices they had ever been offered: freedom from constant and debilitating pregnancy and childbirth. For the first time, sexually active women of

---

6. This attitude towards contraception and the single woman was slow to change. In 1974, the law was finally changed to permit birth-control clinics to prescribe the pill to unmarried women, and it was still considered a controversial decision even then.

all classes could choose to have small families – or to remain child-free – thereby giving them more financial and physical control over their lives.

Ever since the beginning of the 20th century, scientists had been striving to create more effective methods of contraception. In the 1910s and 1920s, several important breakthroughs had occurred. New methods of IUD contraception (most popularly the Gräfenberg ring) allowed women to ensure that they remained protected from pregnancy (if not from sexually transmitted infections) even if their sexual partner refused to use condoms. Before the 1920s, condoms had been made of thick vulcanized rubber, but in the 1920s the latex condom was created and became a much more popular choice. Marie Stopes and the doctors in her clinics did not recommend condoms as Stopes believed them "unromantic and unaesthetic"; the usual method of contraception she recommended was the rubber cap – a method of contraception that the woman had complete control over, without needing to rely on a man to prevent pregnancy.

Marie Stopes did not set up her clinics because she was a great pioneer for women's rights – she was a passionate eugenicist who advocated enforceable sterilization for any men or women deemed "unfit" to have children. The eugenics world believed that any physical or mental infirmity should be "bred out" of the human race. In 1920, Stopes had published the book *Radiant Motherhood* in which she criticized "the diseased, the racially negligent, the thriftless, the careless, the feeble-minded, the very lowest and worst members of the community" who, she claimed, produced "stunted, warped and inferior infants".[7] When her son Harry became engaged to a girl who

7. In 1935, Marie Stopes attended a Nazi-approved International Congress for Population Science in Berlin. She was a great admirer of Adolf Hitler, and sent him an affectionately inscribed copy of one of her books just a month before war was declared between Britain and Germany. In 1942, she wrote a poem which contained the verse: "Catholics, Prussians, the Jews and the Russians, all are a curse, or something worse."

wore glasses, she disinherited him and described his decision to have children with someone who had poor eyesight as a "eugenic crime".

The sexual revolution of the 1920s would be echoed in the 1960s with the introduction of the contraceptive pill. Both eras saw a dramatic change in women's fashions – most notably, in both cases, the shortening of hemlines and the fashion for wearing figure-hugging dresses without restrictive corseted underwear – as women embraced the ability to have choice and control over their bodies. The new young woman of the 1920s became known as a "flapper". Dictionary writers are divided about the origin of the word: some claim it meant a fledgling bird just learning to fly, or a general immaturity, while others believe it was more derogatory, derived from a 19th-century term for "prostitute". Many of the older suffragettes saw the "bright young things" of the 1920s and 1930s as irresponsible and foolish; some even went so far as to say that they felt the flapper generation was too silly to merit the vote that the pioneers had fought so hard to achieve. In 1927, the satirical magazine *Punch* explained that the term was being used to denigrate young women for daring to agitate for equal rights:

> *"'Flapper' is the popular press catch-word for an adult woman worker, aged 21 to 30, when it is a question of giving her the vote under the same conditions as men of the same age."*

Chapter Twenty Two

"To the brave women who to-day are fighting for freedom: to the noble women who all down the ages kept the flag flying and looked forward to this day without seeing it: to all women all over the world, of whatever race, or creed, or calling, whether they be with us or against us in this fight, we dedicate this paper."

The dedication printed in *Votes for Women*

B y the end of 1924, Britain had changed considerably and had been through a chaotic amount of political upheaval. The Liberals had fallen out of trust with each other and out of power in Parliament. David Lloyd George had resigned in 1922, following his failure to secure a coalition government with the Conservatives after the general election. The ensuing Conservative government was led by Andrew Bonar Law, but he was forced to resign in May 1923 through ill health (he died from throat cancer in the October), at which point Stanley Baldwin became Prime Minister. He endured a difficult few months in power before his government resigned in January 1924. Many suffragettes and suffragists were thrilled when, at last, the leader of the Labour party made it to Number 10 Downing Street. The country's first Labour Prime Minister was James Ramsay MacDonald – his party was in power for less than a year. By the end of 1924, Stanley Baldwin's Conservative party was once more at the helm. (Ramsay MacDonald would go on to become Prime Minister a second time in 1929, and to remain in post for six years.) In December of that turbulent 1924, Millicent Garrett Fawcett was honoured by the King for her role in politics – she was made a Dame in the New Year's Honours list. In the same year, Annie Kenney published her autobiography, *Memoirs of a Militant.*

Throughout the 1920s, the suffrage movement continued to agitate for change: every successive government was queried about its policies on equal franchise. Many of these initiatives were led by the Six Point Group, a pressure group set up by Lady Rhondda[1] in 1921. She was a suffragette whose father had been granted special permission to leave his hereditary title to his daughter as he had no sons. In 1922, Margaret Haig Thomas, Viscountess Rhondda (to give her her full title) attempted to take her father's seat in the House of Lords; when she was denied the right, purely because of her gender, she attempted to change the law, citing the Sex Disqualification Act of 1919. Despite a landmark legal case which she seemed to be winning, she was ultimately unsuccessful. Female peers were not admitted to the House of Lord until the 1950s.

As its name implied, the Six Point Group had very specific aims, and about these points Lady Rhondda and her supporters persistently lobbied Parliament:

1) satisfactory legislation on child assault
2) satisfactory legislation for the widowed mother
3) satisfactory legislation for the unmarried mother and her child
4) equal rights of guardianship for married parents
5) equal pay for teachers
6) equal opportunities for men and women in the civil service

---

1. Lady Rhondda would later become the first female president of the Institute of Directors.

The *Evening Telegraph* described it as "the Six Point Group ... which concerns itself with straightening out those parts of the social system muddled or neglected by man" (22 May 1922). Lady Rhondda also set up a new feminist newspaper, *Time and Tide*.

In her autobiographical book *Testament of Youth*, Vera Brittain remembered her first sight of Lady Rhondda, a woman she expected to be "a harsh and pitiless feminist". She was pleasantly surprised: "I was astonished beyond measure at the deprecating sweetness of her expression, the mild earnestness of her hesitating voice, as she spoke rather shyly on the subject of child-assault, which was said to have increased owing to the widespread mental and moral instability that had followed the War." Vera Brittain was so impressed by the charismatic peeress that she started volunteering with the Six Point Group.

In 1926, the year of the General Strike, Lady Rhondda established the Equal Political Rights Demonstration Committee, a pressure group demanding voter equality: for women over 21 to be awarded the vote, just as men over 21 had been. For several years, Emmeline Pankhurst had been absent from the British political scene, having spent much of her time in France, Canada and North America (where she had been in great demand as a speaker). She was back in London for the summer of 1926 when she supported Lady Rhondda's mass meeting in London's Hyde Park – the first large suffrage procession since the end of the war. It was estimated that around 50 organizations and up to 3,000 women attended the event, which for many evoked the nostalgia of their days as young suffragettes. At the head of the procession was carried a banner which proclaimed, "Votes for the Women Left Out". The newspapers made the most of this re-emergence of the old suffragette spirit and the march was reported all over the country. The London correspondent for the *Dundee Courier* wrote that the procession was made up of, "Young, old and middle-aged women. Women in Paris dresses and high-heeled shoes, and women undergraduates in gowns and mortar-boards.... Actresses, Civil Servants, school teachers and the veterans of the fighting days of the Suffragette movement took part. It was a mass of moving colour" (5 July 1926).

One of the oldest people to take part was Charlotte Despard[2], who had gained fame as a militant suffragist and was now, at 82 years old, proud to walk at the head of the procession. In her unpublished memoir, Despard had looked back on her youth and written:

> *"It was a strange time, unsatisfactory, full of ungratified aspirations. I longed ardently to be of some use in the world, but as we were girls with a little money and born into a particular social position, it was not thought necessary that we should do anything but amuse ourselves until the time and the opportunity of marriage came along. 'Better any marriage at all than none,' a foolish old aunt used to say."*

In March 1928, the Representation of the People (Equal Franchise) Bill passed its second reading in the House of Commons. It was passed by a majority of 387 to 10. The Act became law on 2 July 1928. All adults in Britain, male and female, rich and poor, had been enfranchised to vote at the age of 21. Emmeline Pankhurst had lived long enough to see the passing of the Act that she had fought so hard to achieve, but she died on 14 June, before she could hear the King declare the new law. She died a few days before her 69th birthday, but she looked older than she was, her health worn down by the years of prison and hunger striking. One obituary writer commented: "In private conversation she was very gentle. Those who met her thus could never quite understand how this quiet and courteous woman ever came to be the head of the suffragette army. But under that gentleness there was the iron will of the autocrat."

---

2. Charlotte Despard was also famed for being a vegetarian. In another of her campaigns, she railed against vivisection, at a time when few people understood what the word meant.

Millicent Garrett Fawcett died the following year, on 5 August 1929, at the age of 82. An obituary proclaimed: "With the death of Dame Millicent Fawcett there passes from us the last of a small group of women whose life and work have revolutionised the political, social, and ethical state, not of their own country alone, but of the civilised world."

She died in the year in which Britain held its very first general election at which men and women could vote on equal terms. The general election of 1929 became known as the "flapper election" because of the number of fashionable young women seen queuing up to vote. *The Times* announced that the new bill had enfranchised 5,240,000 more voters. Britain now had more female voters than male. It had been a century and a half since Mary Wollstonecraft had published *A Vindication of the Rights of Women*, but at last women in Britain had a fully enfranchised voice.

"Other movements towards freedom have aimed at raising the status of a comparatively small group or class. But the women's movement aims at nothing less than raising the status of an entire sex – half the human race – to lift it up to the freedom and valour of womanhood."

Millicent Garrett Fawcett in 1913

Bibliography & Further Information

Acland, Alice, *Caroline Norton*, Constable, 1948

Atkinson, Diane, *The Criminal Conversation of Mrs Norton*, Random House, 2012

Atkinson, Diane, *The Purple, White & Green*, Museum of London, 1992

Atkinson, Diane, *Votes for Women*, Cambridge University Press, 1988

Bartley, Dr Paula, *Emmeline Pankhurst*, Routledge, 2002

Bartley, Dr Paula, *Votes for Women*, Hachette, 2007

Brailsford, Henry Noel and Murray, Jessie, 'The Treatment of the Women's Deputations by Metropolitan Police. Copy of evidence collected by Dr Jessie Murray and Mr H.N. Brailsford and forwarded to the Home Office by the Conciliation Committee for Women Suffrage', Woman's Press, 1911

Central Committee of the National Society for Women's Suffrage, *Opinions of Women on Women's Suffrage*, London, 1879

Chernock, Arianne, *Men and the Making of Modern British Feminism*, Stanford University Press, 2012

Clifford, Colin, *The Asquiths*, John Murray, 2002

Crawford, Elizabeth T., *The Women's Suffrage Movement: A Reference Guide, 1866-1928*, Routledge, 2001

Cretney, Stephen, *Family Law in the Twentieth Century: A History*, OUP, 2003

Dimand, Robert W. & Nyland, Chris, *The Status of Women in Classical Economic Thought*, Edward Elgar publishing, 2003

Gissing, George, *The Odd Women*, Virago, 1980

Hall, Catherine; McLelland, Keith & Rendall, Jane, *Defining the Victorian Nation*, Cambridge University Press, 2000

Harrison, B.J., *Collection and Preservation of Oral Evidence on the Suffragette and Suffragist Movements*, Social Science Research Council, London, March 1978

Jeffreys, Sheila (ed.), *The Sexuality Debates*, Routledge & Kegan Paul, 1987

Joannou, Maroula, *The Women's Suffrage Movement: New Feminist Perspectives*, Manchester University Press, 2009

Liddington, Jill & Norris Jill, *One Hand Tied Behind Us: The Rise of the Women's Suffrage Movement*, Rivers Oram Press, 2000

Lyndon Shanley, Mary, *Feminism, Marriage and the Law in Victorian England, 1850-1895*, Princeton University Press, 1993

Lytton, Constance and Warton, Jane, *Prisons and Prisoners: Some Personal Experiences*, William Heinemann, 1914

Macdonald, C. (ed.), *The Vote, the Pill and the Demon Drink: a history of feminist writing in New Zealand, 1869-1993*, Bridget Williams Books, 1993

Manton, Jo, *Elizabeth Garrett Anderson*, Methuen, 1965

Mitchell, Sally, *Frances Power Cobbe: Victorian Feminist, Journalist, Reformer*, University of Virginia Press, 2004

Montefiore, Dora, *From a Victorian to a Modern*, 1925

Pankhurst, E. Sylvia, *The Suffragette Movement*, Virago, 1977

Pearsall, Ronald, *The Worm in the Bud: The World of Victorian Sexuality*, Penguin, 1971

Phillips, Melanie, *The Ascent of Woman*, Abacus, 2003
Pugh, Martin, *The Pankhursts*, Penguin, 2001
Pugh, Martin, *The March of the Women...*, OUP, 2002
Rubinstein, David, *A Different World for Women, The Life of Millicent Garrett Fawcett*, Harvester Wheatsheaf, 1991
Smith, Angela K., *Suffrage Discourse in Britain during the First World War*, Ashgate, 2005
Smith, Harold L., *The British Women's Suffrage Campaign 1988-1928*, Pearson, 2009
Stickney Ellis, Sara, *The Women of England: Their Social Duties and Domestic Habits*, Cambridge University Press, 2010
Stopes, Marie, *Married Love*, The Critic & Guide Company, 1918
Strachey, Ray, *Millicent Garrett Fawcett*, John Murray, 1931
Strachey, Ray, *The Cause*, Virago, London, 1978
Vallance, Edward, *A Radical History of Britain*, Little Brown, 2009

WEBSITES:

BBC Archive, Scrapbook for 1912 (bbc.co.uk/archive/suffragettes)
British Newspaper Archives (britishnewspaperarchive.co.uk)
Family Planning Association (Fpa.org.uk)
History of the Labour Party (labour.org.uk)
Liberal Democrat History Group (liberalhistory.org.uk)
Marie Stopes Foundation (Mariestopes.org.uk)
Prime Minister's Office (Number10.gov.uk history-and-tour/past-prime-ministers/)
The Science Museum (Sciencemuseum.org.uk)
UK Parliament Website (Parliament.uk)
Woman and Her Sphere (Womenandhersphere.com)
Women's International League for Peace and Freedom (ukwilpf.org/history)

ARTICLES:

Bartley, Paula, "Suffragettes, Class and Pit-Brow Women", *History Review*, 1999
Bartlett, Jane, 'Force-feeding of hunger-striking suffragettes', *Times Higher Education*, 20 April 1996
Garrett, Elizabeth, L.S.A., "An Enquiry into the Character of the Contagious Diseases Acts of 1866-1869, London, 1870
Hall, John, 'Mental Deficiency – Changing the Outlook', *The Pyschologist*, November 2008
Marquand, David, 'Accidental Hero', *New Statesman*, 6 December 2007
Stack, David, 'A Moment of Madness', *Total Politics*, January 2013

RADIO PROGRAMME:

Great Lives – Series 29, 'John Stuart Mill', BBC Radio 4, 2013

With thanks to the following libraries, museums and archives:
British Library
British Museum
Imperial War Museum
London Library
Museum of London
National Archives at Kew
National Art Library at the V&A
National Gallery
National Portrait Gallery
People's History Museum
Women's Library

Index

Church of England 154, 189
Church League for Women's Suffrage 143
Churchill, Winston 169–71, 169n, 174, 192n
class as factor 17–19, 131–2, 150, 168n
    prison sentences 155–6
clothing reforms 41, 73–81, 241
    Rational Dress movement 73–81
Cobbe, Frances Power 40, 66–8, 70
    animal welfare 67n
    "Wife Torture in England" 66–8
Cobden, Richard 165
Cobden-Sanderson, Anne 135, 140, 165
Collins, Wilkie 43–4
Colmore, Gertrude 204
Conservative Party 62, 63, 93, 99, 142
Contagious Diseases Acts 45–8
contraception 89n, 235–6, 239–41
Cooper, Selina 131, 131n
Cooperative Women's Guild 63
Crane, Walter 85, 86
Cranworth, Lord 33
Crawford, Helen 212
Crippen, Dr Hawley 174n
Crowley, Aleister 164n
Curwen, William 86

Davenport-Hill, Florence 64
Davies, Emily 43, 64
Davison, Emily Wilding 197–206
Dawkins, Lady Bertha 221
Despard, Charlotte 130, 246, 246n
Dickens, Charles 40n, 43, 59n, 74, 90n, 103, 237
divorce
    adultery as grounds 24, 34, 35, 36–7
    children 23–4, 36, 37, 65–6
    cruelty as grounds 34, 35, 36
    domestic violence 37, 66
    equal rights 37
    Marriage and Divorce Bill (1855) 32–5
    Matrimonial Causes Act (1923) 238
    Norton's Letter to the Queen 34–6
    rape as grounds 36
    remarriage following 34, 37
    wife's income 36
Downing Street protest 174, 174n
Drummond, Flora 158, 164, 201
Dublin theatre set alight 171–2
Dugdale, Una Stratford 178
Dunlop, Marion Wallace 154–5
Duveen, Henry 210–11

East London Federation of Suffragettes 207–8
Edinburgh 57

education 42, 52
    campaign for 47n
    Elementary Education Act (1879) 55
    Girton College 41
    medical training 48–9, 65
    Newnham College 47n, 65
Edward VII 47, 112, 121, 175
Eliot, George 41, 58–61, 59n
    Middlemarch 58–61
    "Silly Novels by Lady Novelists" 60
Ellis, Sarah Stickney
    The Women of England 21
Elmy, Elizabeth *See* Wolstenholme, Elizabeth
employment
    agricultural 17–18
    Florence Nightingale 29–32
    generally 18–19
    income from 19, 20, 22–4, 33, 223
    match girls' strike 89–92
    Sex Discrimination Removal Act 238
    Society for the Promotion of the
    Employment of Women 42
    trade union movement 92, 110
    World War I 217–23
English Woman's Journal 41, 42
equal pay 92–3, 244
Equal Political Rights Demonstration
    Committee 245
Ervine, St John 202–3
eugenics 143n, 192n, 240–1, 240n
Evans, Gladys 171

Fabian Society 152
Fawcett family 17
Fawcett, Henry 64, 142
Fawcett, Millicent Garrett 49, 64, 66, 83–4, 104,
    110–11, 116, 122, 134–5, 138–9, 142–3,
    153, 168n, 193–4, 217, 218, 222, 223, 225,
    227–8, 233, 244, 247
    death 247
    "Home and Politics" 83
    Women's Suffrage 177
Female Middle-Class Emigration Society 42
Fish, Henry Smith 96–7
flappers 241
force-feeding 155–9, 187, 192, 198, 212, 214
Ford, Mrs 137–8
Fyfe, Henry Hamilton 87

Garrett, Agnes 139n
Garrett Anderson, Elizabeth 48–9, 65, 146, 163,
    165–9, 228
Garrett Anderson, Louisa 165, 167, 168, 220–1

255

Picture Credits

The publishers would like to thank the following sources for their kind permission to reproduce the pictures in this book.

Plate Section 1
Page 1: (top) Getty Images, (bottom) The Granger Collection/TopFoto; Page 2: Getty Images; Page 3: Hulton Archive/Getty Images; Page 4: Hulton Archive/Getty Images; Page 5: Hulton Archive/Getty Images; Page 6: TopFoto; Page 7: *Regina Cordium* or the *Queen of Hearts*, 1860 (pastel on paper), Rossetti, Dante Charles Gabriel (1828-82)/Private CollectionPhoto/© Peter Nahum at The Leicester Galleries, London/The Bridgeman Art Library; Page 8: (top) Universal Images Group/Getty Images, (bottom) © Illustrated London News Ltd/Mary Evans

Plate Section 2
Page 1: (top) Hulton Archive/Getty Images; (bottom) Hulton Archive/Getty Images; Page 2: (top) Hulton Archive/Getty Images, (bottom) Hulton Archive/Getty Images; Page 3: Popperfoto/Getty Images; Page 4: (top) Hulton Archive/Getty Images, (bottom) Hulton Archive/Getty Images; Page 5: (top) © Underwood & Underwood/Corbis, (bottom) The Women's Library@LSE/© Mary Evans Picture Library; Page 6: (top left) Hulton Archive/Getty Images, (top right) Popperfoto/Getty Images, (bottom) SSPL/Getty Images; Page 7: (top) © Heritage Images/Corbis, (centre) Hulton Archive/Getty Images, (bottom) Hulton Archive/Getty Images; Page 8: (top) © Hulton-Deutsch Collection/Corbis; (bottom) © Illustrated London News/Mary Evans Picture Library

Every effort has been made to acknowledge correctly and contact the source and/or copyright holder of each picture and Carlton Books Limited apologises for any unintentional errors or omissions that will be corrected in future editions of this book.